ARE YOU SITTING COMFORTABLY?

By the same author:

Are you Sitting Comfortably?

MERLIN CAROTHERS

KINGSWAY PUBLICATIONS
EASTBOURNE

ISBN 085476 375 9

Produced by Bookprint Creative Services
P.O. Box 827, BN23 6NX, England for
KINGSWAY PUBLICATIONS
Lottbridge Drove, Eastbourne, E Sussex BN23 6NT
Typeset by J&L Composition Ltd, Filey, North Yorkshire
Printed in Great Britain by Clay's Ltd St Ives plc

Contents

Prelude

When I first began to speak about 'Lukewarm Christians,' I didn't expect to be greeted with much enthusiasm. It's not an easy subject. To my great joy I discovered that Christians *want* to be challenged. The Holy Spirit is inspiring men and women to seek after God's will.

Many, in fact, have asked me for written materials with specific Scriptures to use, as they wake up to God's call to be fully alive and committed to His purposes.

I will do my best to make the subject as palatable as I can, and urge you to hold on to the end. If at any point the message seems too stern, try to picture my happy face, and remember that every word in this book is meant to bless you both now and in eternity.

Put into practice what you learn in the following pages, and in heaven you will say, 'Merlin, thank you for helping me to understand that I could enter into God's secret place, and bring many people to heaven with me.'

1

Please Entertain Me!

For whom am I toiling, he asked, and why am I depriving myself of enjoyment? (Ecclesiastes 4:8).

I woke up one day feeling the weight of every gray hair on my head. I was tired. Bone tired. So I sank into a cushioned chair, put my feet up and began to count the reasons why I deserved to stay there. A calculator would have helped. My life had been long, full and far from easy.

Why, if I only counted my time in the service of my country, I surely deserved to be at ease for the rest of my life!

First there was World War II, as an infantry soldier. Most of my friends in the 82nd Airborne Division hadn't even made it home after those terrible years of battle.

Then, as a chaplain there was Korea, the Dominican Republic and Vietnam. Years of toil in bitter cold and boiling heat. Years of fighting fear, mosquitoes, bugs and all kinds of disease. Years of seeing death and destruction. Years of traveling non-stop, country to country, coast to coast.

I began to add up all my long years of preaching and Bible study, preparation and service. Then there were the ten books I had produced and seen through to publication. I had been working from morning till night, seven days a week for most of my life!

Yes, I had definitely earned time off for good behavior. So began my quest for rest.

First I discovered what it was like to work six days a week. One day off! That was great. Why hadn't I tried that before? Maybe I wouldn't have become quite so exhausted if I had followed God's command to rest one day a week. In fact, I probably needed to make up for lost time!

Since one day off hadn't caused any great calamity, I tried two days off each week. That was even better. Eventually I worked my way up (or down) to six days a week off. Well, not really six days off. I worked at least four hours every day, but at a relaxed pace. And I enjoyed it.

For the first time in my life I got up in the morning when I felt like getting up. Pure luxury. Many people just dream of that day. I went to work when I felt like it. That's the way to work! And I left work when I felt like leaving.

In spite of my comparatively easy life, I took note that I was still having a major impact on the world. I had my books translated and published in thirty-six languages. It wasn't really necessary to work constantly!

Through the Foundation of Praise I was able to send free books every month to thousands of prisoners, military personnel, and hospital patients. Yet I was only working at half speed. After all, I was old, gray haired and tired. I deserved to rest!

And rest is far better, I soon discovered, when it is properly equipped. So my wife, Mary, and I bought two beautiful easy chairs—the kind with vibrators that sooth you to sleep.

When I finished at the office—early—I went home to do my spiritual exercises. An easy chair is a good place for relaxed Bible reading. Being a devoted man, I never failed to read at least a chapter a day. Then it was time to pray.

'Lord, I thank You for the wonderful life You have given me. Thank You for letting me live long enough to enjoy this time of rest. Thank You for a comfortable home, a beautiful and loving wife, healthy children and grandchildren. Most of all, thank You that I'm going to heaven.' By that time, as you can imagine, I became quite drowsy and drifted off for my afternoon nap.

And dozing off, I was completely unaware that I had become like the man Jesus talked about in Luke 12:19:

> I will say to my soul, Soul, thou hast much goods laid up for many years; take thine ease, eat, drink, and be merry (KJV).

When awake, I congratulated myself for finding a variety of ways to enjoy the good life. For all relaxation is not done in easy chairs, you know! I had missed a lot of fun over the years.

So I purchased the plane I had always dreamed of having—a 200 mile per hour, fully instrumented Mooney. What a thing of beauty. What luxury. Punch a few numbers into the computer and it would fly to any place in the United States, Canada or Mexico. All my life I had wanted the time and opportunity to fly. Now I had it!

Motorcycle riding had always been another of my favorite ways to relax. So I bought a Yamaha, Verago 750. What a way to unwind!

For exercise, I brushed up on my golf game and prepared to enter the retiree class of men who love golf. They play seven days a week, rain or shine, and that sounded good to me. After all, earning my livelihood had always taken seven days. I had worked nearly every day of my life since I was fourteen years old. Surely this old man had earned his rest and recreational rights!

I won't fatigue you with my efforts to learn bridge. That is a game so challenging that I could play it constantly, without ever getting bored.

The point is, things were going well. I was throwing myself into rest and recreation with zeal. I had convinced myself that I deserved to be entertained. I had not been balanced in my work, and so—to balance things—I would be equally unbalanced in my rest.

2

The Wake Up Call

*Wake up, O sleeper, rise from the dead, and Christ will
shine on you* (Ephesians 5:14).

One afternoon I was lounging in my easy chair,
sipping a frosty glass of iced tea, when I heard,

'Merlin, what are you doing?'

Startled, but not upset, I answered, 'Lord, I'm just
sitting here thinking about all the good things You have
done for me.'

'You are a lukewarm Christian.'

I felt as if I were being picked up by my right ear and
suspended in mid air. God had my attention! Fear
trembled through my body. Questions swirled about my
head.

Lukewarm? Me? How could that be? I had worked all
my life, and harder than most. But now was not the time
to argue. Something was terribly wrong with me, but I
didn't know what.

'God, what do You mean?'

'I know your works. They are neither cold nor hot.'

I couldn't argue with that. Most of my life my works
had been what I would call 'hot.' Work was second
nature to me. Now I was an old man. I was over the
hill, and surely it was time to rest.

What do You want me to do, Lord?' There was no
answer. He had said what He wanted to say.

The days that followed were long and anguished. Guilt
filled my thoughts from morning to night, but strangely,

13

I couldn't decide exactly what I had done wrong! I was lukewarm, no doubt of it, for the Lord had told me. But what should I do about it?

Perhaps I should go back to preaching. But that seemed out of the question. Part of my burnout had been the near loss of my voice. Speaking for more than ten minutes caused my throat to ache. Doctors determined that if I could go back and delete forty-plus years of preaching two and three times a day, my voice would be cured.

Should I start a new church? That was the last thing I wanted to do, but whatever God wanted was going to have to take first place. Living with this conviction was far too painful.

Examining my heart, I asked the Lord to show me where I had gone wrong. Memories—patterns—of my Christian life began to surface. Seasons of intense spiritual zeal had inevitably been followed by times of pulling back. When I was less zealous, my joy always declined.

What had caused these times of spiritual diminishment? I had thought I was simply resting. Had I relaxed my hold on some stablizing truth or discipline? To my knowledge I hadn't fallen into any sins, at least none that I could think of.

After many tears, and much fasting and repentance, the Lord answered my cries and spoke to me.

'Go back and learn how to pray again.'

'Lord, I haven't stopped praying!'

'Yes, I have seen you praying in your easy chair. Pray like My Son did.'

What did He mean by that? How did Jesus pray?

My search began. What I discovered wasn't what I wanted to find!

> Very early in the morning, while it was still dark, Jesus got up, left the house and went off to a solitary place, where he prayed (Mark 1:35).

After working fifty years to earn the right to retire, getting up in the dark wasn't an idea I wanted to nurture. Twenty years of service as an Army Chaplain had shown me all of the sunrises I ever hoped to see. Now I must relearn how, and apparently when, to pray. Unfortunately, it was beginning to sound like God was in the army too!

Obediently I said, 'Lord, please wake me up at the right time tomorrow so I can pray.' (Maybe He won't and I can sleep in.) The next morning I awakened when it was still dark. Okay then, time to get up.

Mary was still asleep so I did my best to slip out of bed without disturbing her. This was the moment when I learned the difference between a young man getting up to pray at 4.00 a.m. (as I had done years earlier), and an old man trying to do the same. Old joints don't 'slip,' they creak, crack and groan!

Using the early morning braille system, I somehow got into my clothes and made it out the door. Jesus had gotten up and gone outdoors to pray, so that was what I needed to do. He sometimes went up into the mountains to pray, so I chose a hill that is behind our home.

At the top of the hill I paused and prepared to pray. 'Lord, I'm here, but I don't feel like praying. When I'm this tired how can I talk with You in a way that would please You?'

After a painful struggle I gave up and went back home. 'Lord, this isn't going to work. I'm too old to pray like I used to. I don't have the youthful enthusiasm I once had. What am I to do?' No answer. . . .

Back up the hill the next morning—cold, tired, confused—but I knew I had to keep on until the Lord showed me what to do. Morning after morning I got up in the darkness and headed back up the hill. Often I was tempted to give up. And God was surely right about my lukewarm state, for my prayers were lukewarm, no

matter how hard I tried to be filled with the Holy Spirit
and His power.

In Matthew 26:40–41, I saw something Jesus had said
to His disciples when He found them asleep:

> Could you not watch with me one hour? Watch and pray,
> that you enter not into temptation: the spirit indeed is
> willing, but the flesh is weak.

I let that sink in. One hour of prayer, just to be
victorious over temptation! Jesus saw this need, but
apparently the disciples didn't. Jesus prayed. They slept.
God had revealed that His disciples needed to store up
'prayer power' as they would soon be severely tempted.

I live in the same difficult world. Could it be possible
that even an old retired man needed to relearn how to
pray for an hour just to face the day victoriously?

When Jesus told his disciples that their spirits were
willing, I had always thought He was giving them a
compliment. Now I saw that He wasn't. A willing spirit
isn't enough. Many Christians are willing, but we need
to learn how to have strong spirits—strong enough to
do battle with the flesh.

The flesh always wants to control the spirit. Never
had I known that more keenly than in those pre-dawn
wake-up struggles. Our bodies' natural desires want to
tell us when and how to pray. But the flesh never leads
us in the right direction.

I also took note that Jesus' prayers were always
answered, so I needed to learn how He prayed. Hebrews
5–7 reminded me that:

> While Christ was here on earth he pleaded with God,
> praying with tears and agony of soul . . . And God heard
> his prayers because of his strong desire to obey God at all
> times (TLB).

So Jesus prayed earnestly, and with a heart set to obey.
That was the kind of praying I had to relearn. To do

that, my heart had to awaken to the reality of God and His power.

David came to know God and experience His rescuing power through persistent prayer. God permitted him to get into situations where his only choices were: learn or perish. So David said:

> I rise before dawn and cry for help (Psalm 119:147)

Yes, I decided, there must be something important about getting up early in the morning to pray. The flesh doesn't like it, and it will always groan and complain. Sorry flesh, you have had your way long enough.

Then the morning of awakening came. While standing on the top of the hill and looking into the dark sky, heaven opened.

It was as if lightning penetrated my heart. Fire flamed brilliant hot in my breast. I was alive again—I mean really alive! I felt as if I had been translated into heaven. The hilltop became a launching site! Now I had wings to soar like an eagle:

> They that wait upon the LORD shall renew their strength; they shall mount up with wings as eagles; they shall run, and not be weary; and they shall walk, and not faint (Isaiah 40:31 KJV).

This verse became a living reality within me. There wasn't anything I couldn't do. The tired, weary Merlin Carothers was gone. God had swept me back into His arms. The guilt vanished, and a double portion of joy filled my heart. Was I ever awake now!

3

So Much To Learn

Teach me your ways so I may know you and continue to find favor with you (Exodus 33:13).

'Now I'm ready, God! What do You want me to do?'

All I could think of was, I want to serve You Lord. There is nothing else I want. Though I meant that, there was still a great deal yet to learn!

The Lord told me to get back into His Word. He had observed my lazy afternoon readings, and He had other plans for me. I needed to get back to those early days when I studied the Bible at every opportunity. The Spirit showed me that in my lukewarm state I had been content to begin each day with the morning paper. No more!

He showed me that verses such as Matthew 6:33, were to be followed:

Seek ye first the kingdom of God, and his righteousness.

I needed to relearn the importance of beginning each day with not only prayer, but Bible study. And above all, it was important that I want fellowship with Him more than I wanted anything else.

It had become easy to think, after many years of reading and preaching from the Bible, Well I know what's there, so I'll just enjoy reading God's Word in a relaxed comfortable way. That's recreational reading—the sort that goes well in an easy chair, prior to taking a nap!

I went back to the Scripture as if my life depended on uncovering everything there for me. I discovered that:

The eyes of the Lord range throughout the earth to strengthen those whose hearts are fully committed to him . . . (II Chronicles 16:9).

This explained why I had become so weak. I hadn't been fully committed to serving God. Yes, I had been serving Him, but I needed to learn to live out God's definition of 'fully committed.' Perhaps there would prove to be many things that I had never learned. There were.

There was Psalm 119:2:

Blessed are they who . . . seek him with all their heart.

That was exactly what I needed to do. If I sought Him with all my heart, think of what could happen! 'Lord, teach me how to do this! I'll fail if You don't help me.'

The Lord faithfully led me to what is probably the oldest book of the Bible and showed me Job's healthy appetite for the eternal. Job said:

I have treasured the words of his mouth more than my daily bread (Job 23:12).

Now that would require changes in my priorities. Studying first, then eating. Job did more than think about God's words, he savored them. He devoured them like a starving man!

Money, and the wonderful and entertaining things it can buy, has a way of evoking passion in most of our hearts, but God showed me that He wants His Words to stir such emotions. Psalm 119:72 (RSV) says:

The law of thy mouth is better to me than thousands of gold and silver pieces.

Real wealth and prosperity would be found in the treasure of God's Word. But only if I obeyed what I read:

Do not let this Book of the Law depart from your mouth; mediate on it day and night, so that you may be careful to do everything written in it. Then you will be prosperous and successful (Joshua 1:8).

I found that David loved Bible study:

> Oh, how I love your law! I meditate on it all day long (Psalm 119:97).

Why would anyone want to meditate on the Bible all day? I discovered an excellent reason in II Timothy 3:16:

> All Scripture is God-breathed and is useful for teaching, rebuking, correcting and training in righteousness.

Here was another excellent reason for the weakness I had been experiencing. The Bible is God's breath, and if we fail to breathe His breath we become weaklings! God's living breath is mentioned on several important occasions:

> And the LORD God formed man of the dust of the ground, and breathed into his nostrils the breath of life; and man became a living soul (Genesis 2:7 KJV).

> The spirit of God hath made me, and the breath of the Almighty hath given me life (Job 33:4 KJV).

Our bodies had no life until God breathed into us. Now we are given the opportunity to have that life giving breath come into us, daily, through His Word—a constantly available supply! If only I had understood this years ago. I wondered how many other Christians were failing to practice this all important 'spiritual respiration.'

We would all do well to notice what Jesus did when He told the disciples He was sending them out to give the Good News to the world:

> He breathed on them, and saith unto them, Receive ye the Holy Ghost (John 20:22 KJV).

The disciples had the responsibility to take the Gospel to the world, so that required Jesus' breath—His Spirit. I have the same responsibility and the same requirement!

There was another crucial reason why I needed to study the Bible. Hebrews 5:14 says:

> The mature, by constant use have trained themselves to distinguish good from evil.

God's Word, used continually, teaches us what is right and wrong. I hadn't been breathing His Word in regularly, as I did oxygen for my lungs, so I had lost my way. Most adult Christians feel they have been around long enough to know what is right and wrong. That's what I thought, but I was mistaken. Without God's breath, coming into me through His Word, I wasn't able to distinguish between right and wrong.

But as I filled my thoughts and mind with Scripture, I was learning new things. And I fully expected it would continue to be a challenging, exciting journey.

4

What Are You Doing?

Whatever you do, do it all for the glory of God (I Corinthians 10:31).

Now that I was getting up early and working full speed all day, I came home tired—and with good reason. I lay back in my easy chair and picked up a little black box that I kept by my chair. With the push of a button a beautiful scene flashed in front of me.

That's right, television.

'Merlin, what are you doing?'

There was no mistaking God's silent, penetrating voice.

'Oh, Lord, I'm resting. I'm tired. If I watch television for a little while I'll be ready to go back to work.'

'Read I Corinthians 10:31.'

> Whether therefore ye eat, or drink, or whatsoever ye do, do all to the glory of God (KJV).

That verse was familiar to me, but I hadn't thought about it for a long while. What relevance did it have to what I was doing? I wasn't watching anything bad. This isn't x-rated trash, Lord.

'Turn it off.'

That was clear enough, so off it went. There wasn't anything good on that night, anyhow. It wouldn't hurt me to do without TV for one evening, but I sure wanted to watch the next night. My favorite program was on then, and I never missed it. Of course there were some things on the program that I didn't approve of, but it was my kind of plot. It had the bad guy, heroes, drama, intrigue and excitement.

The next evening I was all set to enjoy my show when I heard,

'Merlin, what are you doing?'

'Lord, I'm just watching my favorite program. When it's over I'll be rested and then I will go back to work.'

'Study I Corinthians 10:31.'

So I turned the TV off and studied the verse. What did it have to do with my watching television? Did it mean I could never watch TV? The Lord would have to do some powerful convincing to persuade me to never watch television again.

'Whatever you do.' That was plain enough. TV was part of 'whatever.' But was I hearing the Lord right? I didn't want to become a fanatic, but I kept having a feeling that there was far more at stake than I realized.

I was going to have to decide what to do with TV. To say that this wasn't an easy question for me, is an understatement. For some people, watching TV is no big thing, but to me it was a very big thing. I could watch it every evening for several hours, or even longer if something good was on. For many years I didn't have time to sit around watching anything. But now I had time! Surely the Lord wouldn't tell a retired old man that he had to give up a harmless pleasure.

'Whether you eat or drink,' the verse had said. That covered most of the pleasures people had when those words were written. And God was telling the church at Corinth, 'Even your most common pleasure must be dedicated to My glory.'

That meant my television watching had to be dedicated to God's glory. Before I could turn on my favorite program I would need to read the Bible, pray and then tell Him that I would be watching TV for Him. How in the world could I do that?

'I understand, Lord, no more of my favorite show. It isn't a good choice. So what programs can I watch?'

'Search My Word.'

It was easy to know that God was speaking to me. Satan wouldn't tell me to study God's Word. And he most certainly would never suggest that I measure my choices against God's standards. I wasn't relishing what I expected to find:

Avoid every kind of evil (I Thessalonians 5:22).

I can tell you that I didn't like the sound of that verse. Could some of my favorite programs actually be classified as evil? I hadn't really considered the possibility. When my attention hadn't been constantly on God's Word, evil wasn't clear or distinct to me. The line between right and wrong had blurred. But now I was slowly getting a better understanding. Evil is evil, and God is against it. He hates evil.

I remembered reading somewhere that He wants us to hate evil. I found the reference in Amos 5:15 (KJV):

Hate the evil, and love the good.

I thought, How can I hate something that I love? Being an avid TV watcher required me to avoid making any hasty decisions on this matter!

The next evening I turned the tube on, flipping from channel to channel to see what programs seemed to be evil, and if there were any that were good. But before I turned it on I read some pertinent Scriptures, and prayed for understanding. I wanted to know God's will—at least part of me did.

The shows on every channel seemed totally different from what they had previously been. The tone of the programs were wrong; they reeked with anti-Christian attitudes. The sitcoms were anti-authority. Fathers were weak and ignorant. Policemen were corrupt and unworthy of respect. Even the comedies stretched as far as they could to make fun of morality.

Avoid every kind of evil.

'Lord, everything in these programs isn't evil. There must be some shows that are good clean fun.'

I knew that among television's offerings there could be found some valuable educational programs and documentaries. Although they usually deny God as Creator, these shows reveal the wonders, beauty and complexities of this world and universe. But the truth was, the more I searched the regular fare, the more my heart and eyes were opened. Evil was there, but it was dressed up in Hollywood's glamour and appeal.

Long forgotten news items began coming to mind . . . suggestions that the owners, producers, and directors of television and movies have an 'agenda.' And judging by what I was seeing, it is far from a righteous one.

I recalled an estimate that about one hundred men and women control everything that comes to us on commercial television. Their choices have deeply impacted the moral values of our nation. Through their programming they demonstrate a belief that everyone has the right to make up his or her own mind as to what is good, and what is not. Clearly, they see nothing wrong with immorality as the Bible defines it, since that is not their belief system. So they have presented their own form of permissive, pleasure-seeking 'religion' on the silver screen.

While I had been sitting at the feet of these clever, modern day gurus, other men were calling for people to wake up to this trend to disguise evil as entertainment. In a feature article in the Miami Herald, John Underwood, a former senior editor for *Sports Illustrated* noted, 'For evil to flourish among otherwise well-intentioned people, it must gain acceptance as something else— something more palatable, something that can deflect the truth. Of course,' he says, 'if we call it entertainment, we can stretch the limits a little.'

It was becoming painfully obvious that my much loved pastime had the power to move even the casual observer toward accepting aberrations and vulgarity, greed and materialism as the norm. As these daily doses of depravity have subtly defiled us, the moral standards of our world have shifted.

I had to admit that each year the bill of fare has pressed on toward ever increasing debauchery while we—God's people—have been resting, retiring and . . . watching! We've been entertained by the show. We have circled our favorites, and programmed them onto our VCR's to avoid missing anything while we go to church.

Without shame or remorse, we have watched programs in which a couple meet and in one evening jump into bed together, as if that were quite normal.

'Hard to believe, isn't it,' writes David N. Rosenthal in an article in the *San Diego Union*, October 9, 1991, 'that once you couldn't even say the word "pregnant" on TV or put two married people in the same bed, let alone two unmarried people.'

Yet today, parents sit and watch immorality in the same room with their children, and no longer feel embarrassed. God, help us! We have lost our conscience. I had certainly lost mine. How the angels must weep.

Then I found a verse that seemed to be the cornerstone of God's eternal position on what Christians should or should not do. It is II Timothy 2:19:

> God's solid foundation stands firm, sealed with this inscription: The Lord knows those who are his, and, Everyone who confesses the name of the Lord must turn away from wickedness.

What a verse! God's place to start—everything He builds on—is the foundational truth that every person who works with, and for Him, must separate himself from wickedness. Whoever tries to do anything in His name, must do it according to this foundation, for His rule is firm and unyielding.

Everyone who says he is a Christian has something that he must do. It was becoming clearer to me what I must do. I must turn away from wickedness. If I failed to do that, I could not expect to build on God's foundation. If I wanted the benefits that He promised in His Word, I had to learn what was wicked in His eyes, and then turn away from it.

When I watched television I was continuously facing violence, sensuality, and a mocking of nearly everything God calls us to do and be. Well, if television was evil, then I guess I would have to face it in the opposite direction.

5

The Struggle

In your struggle against sin, you have not yet resisted to the point of shedding your blood (Hebrews 12:4).

What a painful thought it was to consider giving up television viewing! (Like shedding my blood!) If anyone ever had a 'sacred cow,' I did. My hallowed pleasures were movies and TV, and I earnestly did not want to part with them.

Previously I had heard our eight year old granddaughter ask, 'Grammy, why does Grandpa watch TV so much?' That made me angry. I thought, Why doesn't her mother teach her better manners? I've since learned that we usually do get angry when anyone criticizes our 'sacred cows'—whatever they may be. In the devotional booklet, 'Our Daily Bread,' I once read that, 'The more a person is addicted to a vice, the less he cares for advice!' That certainly had been true for me.

Gradually I came to realize that God didn't just want to turn me away from something I enjoyed. He wanted to turn me away from what would contaminate me, so that He could turn me toward His best and highest purpose.

In II Timothy 2:20–21 TLB, He explains:

> In a wealthy home there are dishes made of gold and silver as well as some made from wood and clay. The expensive dishes are used for guests, and the cheap ones are used in the kitchen or to put garbage in. If you stay away from sin you will be like one of these dishes made of purest gold—

the very best in the house—so that Christ himself can use you for his highest purposes.

It was up to me to decide what purpose I wanted to fulfill in God's house. I had a feeling that my decision would be not only for this world, but also for the next age! Now, that is heavy!

Through my service to God, I could be likened to gold and silver, or wood and clay. Of course wood and clay have value, as does every Christian, but gold and silver are in a different category of service. They are far more useful to the Master than clay. Clay is of plentiful supply. Anyone can find it and use it.

The most interesting part of these verses is that they reveal that a child of God can, by his own choice, avoid what would defile him and thus actually choose to be used for some higher, holier purpose! God doesn't force us into higher service, either for now or for eternity. Yet how utterly foolish I would be, I realized, to choose temporary pleasure now, when I could have an eternal place of special service to God.

Too many of us have the perception that if we can just make it to heaven, that is more than enough. What a limited perspective! When I get to heaven I want to rejoice in every person I have helped bring to Christ. That will be as enjoyable as being there myself! God promises to reward every one of us according to the good we have done. (II Corinthians 5)

That is not to imply, however, that we get to heaven by good works! Titus 3:5 reminds us that it is:

Not by works of righteousness which we have done, but according to his mercy he saved us (KJV).

It is only after we receive God's merciful salvation through Jesus Christ that we are able to do work that is truly good.

Well, I was a grateful recipient of His mercy, and I found myself earnestly wanting to do good works. But something stood in the way. Could it be, I wondered, my preoccupation with pampering and pleasing myself?

In II Timothy 3:1–2, 4, I found:

> There will be terrible times in the last days. People will be lovers of themselves . . . lovers of pleasure rather than lovers of God.

Is that what had happened to me? Like it or not I had to find out what sort of Christian Merlin Carothers was.

'A lover of pleasure more than a lover of God.' Is that how God saw me? If so, it was time to take a good look at myself.

If I had the choice of watching TV or preaching the Good News of the Gospel, which would I prefer? No matter what I might claim, the fact was that my recent years spoke eloquently of what I enjoyed most. Staying home to watch TV was far more enjoyable than preaching, or listening to someone else preach.

Admitting this was difficult. I rationalized in my mind, After preaching for so many years it is impossible for me to hear another preacher without picking apart everything he says. If I'm going to do that I'm better off to stay at home. Mary and I went to church on Sunday morning, but that was the most I wanted to do.

What had caused me to have such a dreadful attitude? Much of my life I had loved going to church! I loved prayer meetings, revival meetings and Bible studies. What had caused me to prefer sitting at home watching an impersonal little box of moving pictures?

I had a dozen reasons that I could give, but they were all boiling down to one fact. I was part of the 'terrible times' that God said would come upon us in the last days. Men would love pleasure more than God.

It was easy for me to think, It's not God I'm rejecting. I love Him. It's the forms of religion that I don't like. But what I thought, wasn't important. God had told me I was a lukewarm Christian. And now He was shining

His light on my preference to sit before the world's entertainment rather than to bow before Him in worship.

Perhaps I needed to view television through God's eyes. Surely God sees more than bright colors, beautiful people, and fascinating programs. In Proverbs 8:13 (KJV), He teaches the wisdom of looking beneath what may be an appealing surface to what is being represented:

> If anyone respects and fears God, he will hate evil. For wisdom hates pride, arrogance, corruption and deceit of every kind.

That was something to mull over. How much pride, arrogance, corruption and deceit do actors project on TV and movies? What percentage of TV and movies manifest those behaviors? Previously I hadn't given those fine points much thought.

One day during devotions I said the Lord's Prayer. One phrase leapt out at me:

> Lead us not into temptation (Matthew 6:13 KJV).

How could I pray, 'lead me not into temptation,' if I was facing temptation and enjoying it? I didn't think it would work to change the Lord's Prayer to, 'Lead me not into temptation, because I'm already leading myself into all the temptation I can handle!'

Is it possible, I wondered, to enjoy being tempted? I recalled hearing of a study that television producers made to learn how men react when they see a gorgeous woman on TV. Cameras were focused on men's eyes as they watched television programs. Without exception, when a man saw a seductive looking woman on the screen, the pupils of his eyes enlarged! Was he being tempted? Of course he was.

A Christian man might respond with, 'Sure I was tempted, but I didn't give in to it.' That's good, but how much temptation can a Christian withstand? On some days perhaps a lot; on other days perhaps not so much. A better question might be: is there any amount of temptation to which a Christian should deliberately subject him or herself?

During my time in the military I frequently saw non-Christian men watch beautiful, alluring women on a movie screen, and then announce, 'I'm going out to find a woman.'

The Christian man would say to himself, 'I'm not going to do that.' He would say that ten times, or a hundred, or a thousand times. But sometimes he, too, reached the point where he gave in to temptation. He might not intend to go out and 'find a woman,' but through subjecting himself to repeated temptation, an erosion of his commitment and obedience to God slowly developed. The old statement is true. 'What goes in—comes out.'

Jesus put it this way:

If the light that is in you is darkness, how great is that darkness! (Matthew 6:23 KJV).

If I feed darkness into my mind, then the light in me becomes darkness. Could that be the reason, I wondered, for the spiritual lethargy that I had sometimes experienced? The only reason? Perhaps there were other things of which I still wasn't aware. I needed to keep digging into God's Word for every secret I could find.

In Ephesians 5:10–11, I found another important directive:

Find out what pleases the Lord. Have nothing to do with the fruitless deeds of darkness, but rather expose them.

I needed to find out if God was pleased with anything offered in my TV guide. I needed to find out His system for rating the movies. And if God wouldn't like them, then should I? What programs would Jesus be happy to sit in my living room and watch along with me?

Spiritual darkness does not like to be exposed, I discovered. Especially when it's in me!

How I wish that years ago I had paid closer attention to the things that the Apostle Peter obviously understood when in Acts 4:40, he spoke to his generation:

> He warned them; and he pleaded with them, Save yourselves from this corrupt generation.

Things have gotten no better since then. And I was reluctantly realizing that I had no business feasting on the world's table of corrupt delights just because I could hide in my living room to do it.

6

A Time To Choose

Choose this day whom you will serve (Joshua 24:15 RSV).

I wonder how many of us laughed at the Calvin and Hobbes comic strip the day young Calvin told his tiger friend, Hobbes, about the great science fiction story he had just read where 'machines take control of humans and turn them into zombie slaves!'

Hobbes leaped down from the swing where he had been sitting, grabbed the book and exclaimed, 'So, instead of us controlling machines, they control us? Pretty scary idea.'

'I'll say,' Calvin agreed, and then looking at his wrist watch yelled, 'Hey! What time is it? My TV show is on!'

If we didn't chuckle over that cartoon, it may have been because we were convicted by its truth. It's not funny to realize that we, who call ourselves servants of God, have too often allowed ourselves to become servants of the 'machine' called television. Yet I had certainly become a slave to its programmed influence.

I confess to you that I loved the entertainment this worldly machine produced—the same scintilating entertainment that anti-Christians enjoy. The television was my daily companion—an absorbing friend.

However, it seems that the kinds of people with whom we choose to have fellowship can have a great influence on us. In I Corinthians 15:33. I found Paul saying:

Do not be misled. Bad company corrupts good character. And then he pleads, (verse 34) Come back to your senses as you ought, and stop sinning . . . In II Corinthians 6:14, I found another painful verse:

Do not be yoked together with unbelievers. For what do righteousness and wickedness have in common? Or what fellowship can light have with darkness?

The Holy Spirit reaffirmed that in this day and age, 'fellowship' does, indeed, include those fascinating people who enter my life electronically day after day, influencing me subtly while I relax, unguarded. Previously I had considered TV actors as someone 'out there, somewhere.' More and more I was seeing that I was actually inviting these people into my living room. Other than my wife, they were in my home more than any person on earth!

Movie and television actors have become a class of people unto themselves. By their own declaration, few of them go to church, or believe in Christian values. On virtually every moral and political viewpoint, they stand shoulder to shoulder against God's laws.

Writer-Producer John Prizer was quoted in the *AFA Journal*, Nov/Dec '91, as saying, 'I can't think of a director or actor or writer under 45 who goes to church or synagogue.' What bothers Prizer and others, including movie critic Michael Medved, is that this lack of religious faith is translated into their work.

Ron Austin, a writer and producer of such shows as *Mission Impossible, Charlie's Angels* and *Matlock*, advises us to keep in mind that Hollywood 'is dealing with a mass product for a mass audience. It produces entertainment. They're selling escape from reality and truth. Religion is about truth, and anything tough about life, like the choice between good and evil, is avoided. The real law in Hollywood is money, and if they could sell a religious movie or TV series, they'd sell it—twisted, of course, to fit their theology!'

With this kind of evidence to back up what I could now see all too clearly, I had to admit that, on the whole, these people are not good company for a Christian. But they are beautiful, glamorous and appealing. They have talent, persuasive abilities, zeal and commitment—commitment to their cause; not to God's cause. These are the people I had been spending more of my time with than anyone else. These are the ones I had invited into my life to influence me.

Why had I done this? Did I deliberately intend to displease God? No, I watched TV for one reason—I enjoyed it. It entertained me.

But, until God put His finger on James 4:4, it had never occurred to me that my friendship with the world actually made me God's enemy:

> You adulterous people, the verse says, Don't you know that friendship with the world is hatred toward God? Anyone who chooses to be a friend of the world becomes an enemy of God.

I wasn't foolish enough to think, I will be a friend of God's enemy. Yet He declares that anyone who fellowships with the world is His enemy. I had chosen pleasure from the world's fare, and that choice had put me in the enemy camp according to God's Word. I certainly didn't like that idea, because I knew a few too many things about God's enemy.

Satan caused God's Son to be humiliated, and God hasn't forgotten. Satan caused Jesus' disciples to be brutally murdered, and God hasn't forgotten. Satan has caused unspeakable horrors to be spewed out on God's children, and God hasn't forgotten. God has enemies, and I didn't want to be caught for one minute on their side!

With all my heart, I vowed, I'm going to work against God's enemy. I decided I wanted to be in the same camp with the old Methodist preacher, Uncle Buddy

Robinson, who said, 'I'm going to bite on the Devil for as long as I have teeth, and then I'm going to gum him to death!' Uncle Buddy had a lisp that was so bad people could hardly understand what he was saying. But he preached with great power until he died. Tens of thousands of people accepted Jesus as Savior because Uncle Buddy refused to be a friend of the Devil . . . refused to play in his yard.

Solomon, the wisest man who lived, gave this advice:

> Don't do as the wicked do. Avoid their haunts—turn away, go somewhere else (Proverbs 4:14–15 TLB).

God is asking us to choose whose side we are on, and then move there. It's not possible to stand with one foot in God's kingdom and the other in the world. I John 2:15 says:

> Do not love or cherish the world or the things that are in the world. If anyone loves the world, love for the Father is not in him.

(A look at what unbelievers love to do with their free time gives a good idea of what it means to 'love the things that are in the world'!) But the verse goes on to warn that:

> If any man loves the world, the love of the Father is not in him (KJV).

This was a frightening thought to me. I knew I couldn't survive without God's love. Jesus explained how our affections change in accordance with our focus when He said:

> For where your treasure is, there your heart will be also (Matthew 6:21).

I treasured the world's entertainment, and my heart had followed its treasure. Now God was calling me back to Himself. For too long I had been like the young man who said to his girlfriend, 'You are the most beautiful and lovable creature that God ever made. I love you with everything that is within me. Being with you gives me more joy than anything in this world. I promise you that I am going to be with you two evenings of every week.'

'Oh?' said the young lady, 'and where will you be the other nights?'

'Don't worry about that. I'll just be with another woman to have fun. Her one flaw is that she really hates you, but other than that, we have so many things in common that I enjoy being with her. You have no reason to be disturbed about it. I don't love her.'

No woman on earth would be satisfied with such an arrangement, yet I had treated Almighty God that way! I had been saying, 'I'm sorry, but I do enjoy fellowship with those who rebel against You.'

Now God in His great mercy was calling me to choose Him once again. He was inviting me to be entertained and delighted by Him alone . . . and to choose my friends from among His friends. I had no idea of the thrills that lay ahead for me as I answered His call by choosing, moment-by-moment and day-by-day, to deny myself, pick up my cross and follow Him.

7

Set Free To Joyously Serve

You have been set free from sin and have become slaves to righteousness (Romans 6:18).

Remember the grandchild who asked why Grandpa watched so much television? Once God had my attention, I saw things more clearly and realized I had never prayed with her! That was unacceptable for any Christian grandfather.

The next time I saw her, I said, 'Bridgette, are you going to heaven?'

She looked puzzled and said, 'I don't know.'

'Would you like to know how to get to heaven?'

Bridgette's eyes lit up and she said, 'Oh yes!' So I led her into receiving Jesus as Savior.

What if I had waited until she was much older, and perhaps so enamored by the things of this world that heaven held little appeal?

I didn't pray with her brother, Eric, because he was only four years old. When he and Bridgette were on the way home, she asked him, 'Eric are you going to heaven?'

Eric said, 'Huh?'

'Are you going to heaven?'

'I don't know.' So Bridgette went through the plan of salvation. Eric had not heard me talking with Bridgette, but when he got home he did something quite significant. He called me on the telephone and said without preamble, 'Grandpa, I'm going.'

I had no idea what he meant, so I responded, 'Yes, Eric, where are you going?'

'I'm going.'

'Where are you going, Eric?'

'I'm going to heaven.'

How glad do you think I was at that moment, that I had listened when God told me I was a lukewarm Christian? If I had continued to waste my time on such things as TV, movies and recreation, I would still have gone to heaven, but I would have missed the opportunity to take some very precious people with me.

I began to realize that I had been set free; but my freedom had a purpose. Along with the apostle Paul I could now say:

> Though I am free (to entertain myself whenever I want) and belong to no man, I make myself a slave to everyone, to win as many as possible (I Corinthians 9:19).

The experience with my granddaughter proved to be just the beginning of an ever widening circle of influence. The next day, Bridgette began to quiz her playmates. 'Are you going to heaven?' With considerable persuasion she led one of them to receive Jesus as Savior. Then she decided to talk to her friend's parents. They too had the wonderful opportunity to hear the Good News.

How many opportunities do we miss when our minds are consumed with our own business and the pursuit of pleasure? For too long my indulgent pastimes had crowded out the truth that:

> He died for all so that all who live—having received eternal life from him—might live no longer for themselves, to please themselves, but to spend their lives pleasing Christ (II Corinthians 5:15 TLB).

I am certain that if someone had suggested I needed to get my eyes off the television, I would have ignored them. After all, I knew better than anyone that I deserved my rest and recreation. Someone else's ideas were not enough to move me. It took God's living Word to move me past my self absorption and open my eyes to what I was really watching:

> Get rid of all moral filth, God clearly commanded in James 1:21. And in verse 27, Keep yourself from being polluted by the world.

He goes on to warn:

> . . . Escape the corruption in the world caused by evil desires (II Peter 1:4).
> For he that soweth to his flesh shall of the flesh reap corruption; but he that soweth to the Spirit shall of the Spirit reap life everlasting (Galatians 6:8 KJV).

God's Word is able to speak with power because He made each one of us, and He knows us inside and out. He understands that living for ourselves is as natural as breathing air; we do it without thinking. Still, He calls us to wake up and live for Him. In I Corinthians 6:19–20, He reminds us:

> You are not your own; you were bought at a price.

The price that He paid for us was so high that we, who have been purchased and set free through His own Son's blood, are expected to serve Him. However, being God's servant is hardly work without pay.

God knows that if we live for Jesus we will be spared much unnecessary suffering, and have great eternal joy. He wants us to have 'LIFE,' and He knows how to entertain us!

Jesus said:

> I have come that they may have life, and have it to the full (John 10:10).

That certainly doesn't sound like a God who is trying to take all the fun out of life! But His life cannot be real to us until we tear ourselves away from the entertainment that is designed to turn us away from Him.

I was required to let go of my earthly ideas that said, 'this is really living,' in order to take hold of God's offer of exciting, incredible LIFE that begins now, and lasts through eternity. And was it ever beginning now!

It started on top of the hill early that morning. When the Lord poured His life back into me, I found myself praying with a fervor I hadn't felt in years, shouting, 'God, I'm victorious in Christ! God, You have set me free!' I was weeping, laughing, singing, and being changed each step of the way.

Every day I felt new strength sweeping into my heart. The old tiredness was gone. Passion to build God's Kingdom came back, but in a new dimension. The strength of spirit that I once had, was doubled. At least doubled!

The entertainer can put laughter on our face, but only the Holy Spirit can put a smile in our heart. And my heart was smiling more and more.

> Be delighted with the Lord. Then He will give you all your heart's desires (Psalm 37:4 TLB).

I felt as if I were entering a place I had never before enjoyed. The best way I can describe it is to say that it seemed to be a 'secret place' where wonderful things were happening inside me. Perhaps I was dwelling in the secret place of the Most High—that place of rest, safety, refuge, communion and blessing described in the ninety-first chapter of Psalms.

And the more time I spent there, the more my heart delighted in the Lord and sought after Him. Deuteronomy 4:29 was proving itself in me:

> You will seek the Lord your God, and you will find him, if you search after him with all your heart and with all your soul (RSV).

My heart was telling me that I was seeking more than ever before to know my Father.

I was beginning to understand what He meant in Deuteronomy 6:5:

> Thou shalt love the Lord thy God with all thine heart, and with all thy soul, and with all thy might (KJV).

My heart was responding to Proverbs 3:6:

> In everything you do, put God first, and he will direct you (TLB).

My new blessings were far outweighing the pleasures I had enjoyed when I had 'dwelt' outside God's dwelling place by feeding myself on the world's fare. I didn't see how it could get any better!

8

Sent With A Message

Therefore, go and make disciples of all nations . . . teaching them to obey everything I have commanded you (Matthew 28:19).

One morning I was so full of His Spirit that I thought I could contain no more. I cried out, 'Oh, Lord, what can I do for You?'

There was no way that I could go back to preaching. Not only was my voice too weak, but I had no place to preach. For years when people had called and asked me to speak in California, New York, Europe, Asia, Australia and in dozens of other places, I had always said, 'I'm sorry, but I can't.' That was true because, with my voice problem, I really couldn't.

So I cried, 'Lord, what can I do?'

He was ready with an answer.

'Do what you did when I first called you.'

It was easy to remember what I did, even though it was way back in 1939. I simply spoke to anyone who would listen.

'Okay, Lord, if that's what You want, that's what I'll do.' The first person who came to my mind was one of our neighbors. I thought, He's already a Christian, but by this time I was learning to listen rather than argue. On the way to my neighbor's home, I wondered what he would think when I asked him if he was going to heaven.

As a neighbor, he was perfect: cheerful, always available to help everyone, and he went to church every

Sunday. But when I questioned him about his expectation of being in heaven, he looked a little surprised and said, 'No, I don't believe I'm good enough. I wish I were, but I'm not.'

'Do you know there's a way that you can be sure you're going to heaven?'

'I've always wished I could know that.'

I told him the simple plan of salvation, and as I explained it, tears ran down his cheeks. Everything I told him was news to him. He had never understood the Good News! Soon we prayed together and he received Jesus as his personal Savior. When we were through, his face glowed with a new delight.

Now when I see this neighbor, I say, 'Are you going to heaven?' and he shouts back, 'Yes!' Isn't that glorious?

That brother had been my neighbor for over four years, and I had never talked to him about God's Good News. Why hadn't I? I was too busy being entertained to listen to God's Spirit, or to be about His work.

Then I remembered a car dealer from whom I had purchased a car. The Holy Spirit reminded me that I had not spoken to him about Jesus, so I headed for the garage.

When the salesman was able to talk with me, I asked him the same question, 'Are you going to heaven?' He, too, looked puzzled and answered, 'I don't know.'

As we talked I learned that he had attended a Bible believing church nearly every Sunday of his life. When I asked him what he thought he needed to do to get to heaven, he said,

'I'd have to live better than I do.'

After I explained the Gospel to him, I asked if he had ever heard this in church. Perhaps he had, but he assured me that he couldn't remember ever hearing it. When I asked him if he was sorry for his sins, his face took on an expression of intensity as he said, 'I sure am!'

Right there on the showroom floor we prayed and,

with tears of repentance, he accepted Jesus as Savior and Lord.

Jesus pleads with us in John 4:35:

> I tell you, open your eyes and look at the fields! They are ripe for harvest.

My neighbor, and that salesman were part of the Holy Spirit's 'ripe and ready fields.' God needed someone willing to harvest for Him . . . someone whose eyes were not fastened to the silver screen . . . someone whose ears were not constantly enchanted by this world's sounds. But Jesus knows that many of us are content to be 'part-time followers.' Surely it breaks His heart.

He continues to say, as He said in Matthew 9:37:

The harvest is plentiful. (For His Spirit is always faithful to do the Father's work.) But the workers are few. (Far too many of us are out playing and resting in the fields as the ripe grain falls to the ground.)

So I continued telling the Good News to anyone who would listen—in restaurants, the bank, and many other places. Not everyone responded positively. But that was fine, since I knew responsive hearts had been ripened by the Spirit, and the rest of the time I was planting important seeds. My spirit soared on wings like an eagle!

One morning I awakened with a great desire to preach. For many years I had yearned for the time when I would no longer have that responsibility. Some men deliver God's message with a relaxed ease, but my calling required me to preach as if I needed to convince every person to make a life-changing decision. This had always left me exhausted.

Now here I was, retired, and wanting to preach again! But how could I, with my pathetically weak voice? 'Lord, what should I do?'

Loud and clear His answer came to my spirit,

'You speak. I will take care of your voice.'

And so I began to call and write to the places that had, over the years, invited me to speak. Many of them said, 'Come as soon as you can.'

One day while I was driving to work, I sensed the leading of the Spirit to speak, out loud, right there in the car. Then I heard,

'Speak up! Speak up toward the stars.'

I thought, What does that mean? Well, for whatever reason, I'd better speak to the stars. so I drove along calling out to the stars, feeling very strange indeed!

After a few shouts, I noticed that my voice sounded altered. No matter how loudly I shouted, my throat didn't hurt! So I continued shouting prayers and praise.

Something was happening to me. After forty-nine years of living with a voice that got weaker with each passing year, it was now stronger than it had ever been! But—perhaps I'm a direct descendant of 'Doubting Thomas'!—I couldn't help wondering how long it would last.

When I went places to minister, my voice took on a completely new quality. Not only was there more volume, but I spoke with a new ring of authority. I often felt as if God was speaking through me. In previous years I had experienced a similar feeling, but now it was increasingly strong. People who had heard me speak over the previous twenty years said, 'Merlin, you have more zeal and power than ever before!'

All of this left me with a new problem . . . perhaps the same problem the Apostle Paul had when he preached until a man fell asleep and tumbled out the window to his death. It was so easy to speak that I wanted to talk on and on!

Now it became necessary to watch the congregation to be sure I wasn't wearing them out (the Apostle Paul brought his 'sleeping' congregant back to life, but I didn't think my faith was quite up to that yet!)

The Lord told me that my latter years were going to

be more fruitful than any of my previous years. So I stayed out of my easy chair and labored for His Kingdom. What delight I was finding in His work!

However, I did have one problem. Before each speaking opportunity I wrestled with the question of what I should talk about. People expected to hear about praise, because that had been my subject for years. Should I continue that ministry, or should I address lukewarm Christians? The Holy Spirit kept insisting that He wanted me to call God's people to 'discipleship.'

If this meant what I thought it meant, I was concerned. I knew from my own experience that people don't want to be told what they don't want to hear. God had worked long and hard to convince me to pull away from my entanglement with the attractive things of this world.

It had been anything but easy to give up my pleasures. I hadn't wanted to hate what I so fervently loved. And I certainly didn't want to become a fanatic about these things. But God had called me to become a committed disciple.

Now He was calling me to deliver a hard message to His people. There was a sense of urgency that overrode my reluctance.

I decided it was fortunate that I was retired. If people didn't like what God was telling me to say, at least they couldn't fire me!

9

Unexpected Rewards

They will still bear fruit in old age, they will stay fresh and green, proclaiming, The Lord is upright; he is my Rock (Psalm 92:14–15).

As I did what I believed God was telling me to do, He spoke to me more frequently. One day He reminded me that I could never do more for Him than He would do for me.

'I will always give you twice as much,' He said.

And how true that was. Though I wasn't asking for anything. He continued to give me unexpected blessings. His strength and energy began to touch me in exciting new ways.

For many years, the effort of preaching a sermon would leave me in a state of exhaustion. After most talks, I simply handed the mike to my host, then left by the side door. People often misunderstood such a hasty exit.

It wasn't that I didn't want to stay to greet people and pray for them. I simply felt too tired to do anything more. Dragging myself to the pastor's study, I would collapse, feeling guilty that I couldn't do more for those who attended the meeting.

Even if I had been able to summon the energy to stay for further ministry, I would have been forced to sit down to do it. I seemed to wear out from the bottom up! When I stood for a mere ten minutes, my feet began to protest. Within thirty minutes they were screaming with pain. I tried shoes of all kinds, as well as chiropractors and podiatrists, but nothing helped. It is

53

next to impossible, I discovered, to care about other people's problems when your feet are demanding—and getting—your undivided attention.

But God began to work changes in me. First my voice had come back, then new energy, and finally . . . new feet! Instead of thirty minute sermons, I found myself preaching twice, or even three times that long. Now that my body was no longer a reliable alarm clock, and my heart was overflowing with the messages God was giving me, I needed someone to stop me!

With my new energy and 'wear guaranteed feet,' I began staying afterward and inviting people to come forward so Mary and I could pray with them. Hundreds came. And they were willing to stand in line for hours. Mary and I prayed until midnight, and still my feet didn't hurt. What great joy that gave me!

As we prayed, other miracles happened. People reported being healed. That put new life into this senior citizen! The Devil's pleasures are dust and ashes in comparison to the joy of praying for someone and seeing God heal them.

Healings, however, were not the greatest joy. People by the hundreds came forward to accept Jesus as Savior. Seeing that, was like finding one of my brand new feet had already crossed the threshold into heaven! The voice of the Lord spoke to me:

'Didn't I tell you that you would see more in your latter years than in all your other years?'

'Yes, Lord, I know that's what You said, but I didn't know you meant things as glorious as this.'

And I remembered how I had let this flesh in which I live deceive me for so long, convincing me that I must entertain myself in order to have joy—suggesting that I needed to rest and retire to be happy. Now I was experiencing unbelievable joy and rejuvenation from the Author of joy, Jesus. Only He can give His rewards.

Now I understood what Caleb meant when he said:

Here I am today, eighty-five years old! I am still as strong today as the day Moses sent me out; I'm just as vigorous to go out to battle now as I was then (Joshua 14:10–11).

Forty years earlier, God had told the Jews to march into the Promised Land and possess it in His name. Only two men wanted to go with Moses—Joshua and Caleb. When all the others were afraid, these two men said, 'With God's help, we can do it.' Caleb held fast through all the years the Jews wandered in the wilderness. After forty years God once again said, 'Go, take your inheritance.'

Caleb was ready, and at a robust eight-five years of age he said, 'I followed the Lord my God whole-heartedly.' God likes that kind of spirit, for it is His Spirit—His power—His own energy, coming back to Him in joyful service.

Over one million Israelite men had been afraid to trust God to help them. But two men had said, 'God will keep His word, let's go.'

How encouraging to realize that just one or two people who chose to work for God with their whole heart, could change the course of a nation's history! What was true then, remains true today.

Though Christians today be numbered in the millions or hundreds of millions, only those who are obedient will enter into the promised land of special blessings.

When we realize that our time and energy are valuable, and that God's strength is available to us, God begins to move and work in accordance with His power, not our weakness. How clearly I was experiencing this truth in my life. Yet how little I knew of the extent of His abundant blessings and rewards. God had just begun.

One day Mary and I went to Crestline, California to hear a famous eye surgeon from Brazil. We heard that he had an unusual gift of prophecy. I had a very cautious attitude toward prophets, since I had often heard prophecies that did not come true.

This prophet, Dr. Pedro, stepped up to the pulpit with his interpreter, and quietly waited for the Lord to speak through him. Then he pointed at me and said, 'God says you are not to retire. He has much work for you to do. He has books for you to write.'

When the service was over I went up to speak with him. With some embarrassment at his inability to speak English, he called once again for the interpreter, our dear friend Bob Curry, and asked him to introduce me. After the introduction, Dr. Pedro exploded with surprise and delight. 'You are Merlin Carothers? Your books changed my life!'

Having had no idea who I was, he could hardly believe that God had used him to prophecy to me.

The next morning Mary and I met with Dr. Pedro and his wife. Bob had been with the doctor in Brazil and knew him well. After we had a prayer, and the doctor gave more prophecy, I said to my friend Bob, 'At one time I had the gift of prophecy, but I haven't used it for so long that I may have lost it.'

'Merlin,' Bob said, 'All you have to do is use your faith and God will restore your gift.' Since I have learned to trust Bob's wisdom, I decided to follow his advice. Little did I think that in only a few minutes that gift would be resurrected!

Since the doctor and his wife had been such a blessing to Mary and me, we asked if we could pray for them. Their faces glowed with a clear answer. Mary prayed first, and then prophesied. Her words were something like, 'You have a deep burden, but God says to tell you that He is completely in control, and that He will take care of it.' We had no knowledge of their personal lives nor of any problems they were having.

Then my own faith came alive and I prophesied. 'God tells me that Satan devised an elaborate scheme to seriously wound you. Satan rallied many of his forces to do something evil. It's your child! Satan wants to kill your child. But God says Satan will not succeed. He has come against Satan and will defeat him. Do not be afraid.'

By this time Dr. Pedro and his wife were on their faces, flat on the floor, weeping. What have I done? I wondered. Did I frighten them this badly?

The doctor's wife jumped up and ran out of the room. I've really upset that dear woman, I thought. In about ten minutes she came running back into the room and gave her husband an excited report. The interpreter gave us the message.

'Yesterday, she called Brazil to check on their son. The grandmother said the child had been stricken wth a sudden, severe illness that the doctor couldn't understand. Unable to retain any fluids, he had become extremely weak. The grandmother recommended that the parents come home immediately.

'She has just been on the phone and her mother said, "Something amazing has happened. Your son is completely well!"'

What a way for the gift of prophecy to become active in me again!

Recently when I was praying for a woman, I stopped and told her, 'Something strange is coming to me. The spirit of death is on you.' Then I thought, Oh, Father, please don't let me put fearful thoughts in this lady if it's not You speaking to me.

The woman stood, her mouth wide open with astonishment. 'Yesterday the doctor told me I have cancer,' she said. 'God told you!'

The realization that God had revealed her problem to me, helped reassure this dear woman of her importance to Him. Her faith was strengthened by my words. When I told the spirit of death to leave this woman, she reacted as if a hundred pound load had suddenly been lifted from her shoulders.

Next, a tall refined lady came to me needing help to pray more effectively for her family. She was the only Christian among them, and after praying for years, she was deeply troubled over their lack of response to anything she said or did for them.

After a few moments of prayer, I stopped and said, 'I need to ask you about something before I pray any more. God is telling me that He wants to give you power. Is that okay with you?'

'Oh yes,' she responded, but neither she nor I understood what God was about to do.

I prayed very calmly and quietly that God would give her power to pray for her family. When I finished she stared straight ahead for about one minute. Then she raised a clenched fist and shouted at the top of her voice, 'Power!' Without another word she fell on her face! After a few minutes she leapt to her feet and shouted, 'Wow! Power!' Her friends told me this was completely out of character for her.

Fortunately for all of us, God's power is not bound by our personalities. Whether we are reserved or extroverted, sophisticated or simple, one spark of God's incredible power can land like a jolt of lightening that sets us afire. Or, His strength can come like a quiet steady confidence that grows and cannot be dissuaded. God's abundant strength can come to us in anyway that He chooses. It had certainly been coming to me in exciting new ways.

First, however, I had made the decision to be a full time servant of the living God. I had to choose to turn away from evil in order to turn toward the Source of all purity and power. It took a whole lot of that power, I found, to live the disciplined life of a true disciple!

10

Disciplined Disciples

Then Jesus said to his disciples. If anyone would come after me, he must deny himself and take up his cross and follow me (Matthew 16:24).

'Call people to be my disciples,' God had told me.

Obviously, the call couldn't be dressed up or glossed over with Hollywood glamor or deception. I wasn't going to be allowed to increase the ranks by presenting a message called: 'Easy Street. Enter into God's favor and find fun, food, luxury and leisure!'

My call to disciples could not include suggestions that we might be allowed to get up in the morning when we want to get up, eat what we like, buy whatever we desire, go where we want to go, rest when we feel like it, and enjoy whatever makes us feel good whenever the mood strikes us. I had to tell the truth.

Jesus didn't call us to a life of ease. He called us to get up early, study and work hard, serve selflessly and pray constantly. He warned us to be alert to danger, even when it comes in the form of entertaining distractions.

'Deny yourself,' He said, 'and take up your cross.'

Madison Avenue's executives would sit Jesus down and try to explain the basics of advertising. 'Look,' they'd say, 'never highlight the negatives. Self denial isn't popular this century. Give 'em what they want. It's even okay to create a need if necessary. But for pity sake, don't offer them a cross!

Granted, the idea of a symbol that will always be

associated with you is good thinking, but—a symbol of death lacks a certain promotional appeal. If you hope to achieve any success—you'd better just focus on those heavenly mansions you're building. Heaven . . . blessings . . . peace . . . love . . . joy, those are your best words. Forget the cross.'

But Jesus doesn't watch television or read magazines, so He isn't influenced by commercial advertising techniques. 'Deny yourself,' He calls out again, more firmly, 'Take up your cross and follow me.'

The world's advertising is clever—it's designed to appeal to the masses. Jesus is selective—His requirements attract only a few. He wants disciples who are willing to be like Him. He bore a cross.

> It is enough for the student to be like his teacher, He said, and the servant like his master (Matthew 10:25). He explained further, I have set you an example that you should do as I have done for you (John 13:15).

Our cross, whatever it may be, will always seem heavy. It may be a difficult job, an unhappy marriage, unloving relatives or our own physical characteristics that we dislike. We will be tempted at times, to lay that cross down, but the call is to carry it to our death. We need to have His strength available to do that.

His strength can only come from being in fellowship with Him. II Samuel 22:33 reminds us:

> It is God who arms me with strength.

Just as I had to discipline myself to learn to really pray again, so every true disciple must learn to commune intimately with our Almighty Source of strength. He encourages us by saying:

> Do not fear, for I am with you; do not be dismayed, for I am your God. I will strengthen you and help you; I will uphold you with my righteous right hand (Isaiah 41:10).

I have also learned how much strength comes from feasting on His Word. So as I sound forth the call to discipleship, I am calling you to dig into the Scriptures as I did. In Psalm 119:28 the Psalmist pleads:

Strengthen me according to your word.

In verse 98 he says:

Your commands make me wiser than my enemies, for they are ever with me.

Verse 165:

Great peace have they who love your law, and nothing can make them stumble.

But reading, meditating upon, and understanding God's word takes time. We may have to rearrange our priorities and our schedules in order to be able to commit to a specific hour or more of study each day. We may even need to make ourselves accountable to someone to ensure faithfulness.

But the time may be easier to find than you think. If you recall, God freed up huge blocks of my time by asking me to give up some hallowed pleasures. Some of those pleasures were directly from the enemy's table of delights, and these things clearly had to go if I was going to continue to claim friendship with God. Other pastimes were not inherently evil, but had to be curtailed to make room for the kind of study and meditations that are acceptable in God's sight.

Whenever the suggestion comes to your mind, It's time for me to study the Bible, you may often hear another voice quick on the heels of the first. I don't want to do that. That's the clever tactic of our enemy! He projects such thoughts. He wants to disparage the reality that the Words of Our Creator are the most magnificent and fulfilling we will ever hear or read!

Not long after giving up television viewing, I found

that I needed a new way to unwind at the end of a busy day. I began to eye the section of my bookcase that was filled with all those top notch novels I had been planning to read 'someday'. Someday had arrived at last!

As I was relaxing in my easy chair the next evening, engrossed in one of those well written novels, I heard,

'Merlin, what are you doing?'

'Lord, I'm reading this really great novel that I've been wanting to read for so long.'

'Is the writer a Christian?'

'Well . . . no, I don't believe he's a Christian, but he sure is a good novelist! (I've always enjoyed reading his books. In my opinion he is one of the best.)

Then the Lord directed my attention back to II Corinthians 6:14 (KJV):

> Do not be unequally yoked together with unbelievers . . .

Apparently this was unequally yoking.

Reading the work of secular novelists was not how He wanted me to spend my time and shape my thinking. Fortunately, I had learned by now that when God denied me one thing, He always had something better in mind. I obeyed.

So, what should I do when I needed to relax after a long day's work? If the Lord didn't want me filling my mind with an unbeliever's views of life, then what could I read?

Browsing through my bookcase, I came across some 'old friends' I hadn't enjoyed in years—books by and about my old hero, John Wesley. Some of them I hadn't even completed.

As I read and reread these books about this man of God, my heart surged with understanding. Here was a man who lived the life of a disciple. For over fifty years he began his prayer time at 4 a.m., and preached at 5 a.m., 365 days a year! Why? To him, every moment of every day belonged to God. Years of neglect had caused me to forget the character of the founder of my church, Methodism.

John Wesley had one goal. Preach the Gospel to every creature. To that end he devoted his life. When he was eighty-five years old, his friends begged him not to travel by horse back when it was raining, lest he catch cold. But John wanted to get to another city, to another place, to tell more people how they could be saved through faith in Jesus.

John Wesley called for men of his day to be disciples. He trained anyone who would come under his leadership.

In those days many religious leaders considered it immoral for a man to preach if he didn't have a college degree. 'Not so,' said John, 'Jesus called every man to be a disciple.'

When John considered a man to be ready, he sent him to wherever he thought a preacher was needed. Some of those men made it to a new land, later known as America.

This new brand of preacher blazed many trails across the Colonies. One historian said, 'If you heard something moving in the bush, it was either a bear or a Methodist preacher.' One of those preachers made his way to Wurtemburg, Pennsylvania, and established a little country church. There my father came to know Jesus as Savior, and there his son, Merlin, received Jesus as Lord.

If John Wesley had relaxed and taken life easy, I might never have heard the Good News. Instead, he turned away from a professorship at what was then the most prestigious university in the world. Oxford. He left position, popularity and luxury, to follow his Lord and become a fisher of men.

He believed that we can serve God best if we use 'methods'. For him, methods produced results so he chose whatever methods would help him to tell more people about Christ. When the Church of England rebuffed him and closed their doors to his evangelizing, he went outdoors. Religious leaders considered out-of-door preaching to be sacrilegious, but John preached wherever people would listen.

Soon there were hundreds, then thousands—some of whom traveled for days just to hear him preach. In rain or snow they stood for hours to listen to this 110 pound giant expound on salvation by faith, and about holy living.

If mobs were incited to drive John out of one town, he went on to the next with same message. 'You must believe in Christ as your Savior or you will never reach heaven.'

As I read these accounts, my desire to please God intensified, and I realized how foolish it was to waste my time on entertaining but meaningless novels, or even on magazines filled with rambling about sports, fashions and celebrities. Such materials would do nothing to help me reach other people with the Good News.

The Spirit said to me, 'The decisions you make about how you spend your time will affect many people.' This principle is the same for every Christian. The decisions that you make about how you spend your time will determine the eternal destiny of many people!

11

Redeeming Our Time

See to it, therefore, that you conduct yourselves carefully, not as foolish but as wise people who make the best possible use of their time, because these are evil days (Ephesians 5:15–16 ML).

I believe there is a continual battle between the Kingdom of God and the Kingdom of Darkness for the control of our time. After all, God is not the only one who knows what's important. The enemy understands that how we spend our time defines who and what we are. And he knows that when he steals our time, he has us.

It is difficult for most of us to grasp the value of minutes and hours. They are so daily, so common, so very ordinary. Since we were born, we've had nothing but time, and more time. It's the constant in our lives. We always wake up. The clocks and calendars keep turning. They always have, and it seems that they always will.

As a teen-aged infantry soldier, I perceived time as endless. No matter how many men were killed around me, I knew that my life would go on. But the men who were killed undoubtedly had that same perception. Most young people expect to go on living forever even though some part of their mind knows that isn't true.

It would seem that as we get older we should have a clearer understanding of the certainty of death, but that certainty seems to elude us.

We say, 'Of course I will die. It could happen any time.' But in reality we don't expect to die today. Tomorrow, maybe, but never today. We are tempted to think that however we use our time, today is not all that important. And even if today is important, this next hour can certainly be spared. And before we know it that hour, and the next, and the next, have gone. But, oh well, tomorrow's another day! That's the way the human mind operates. We always expect to have another hour, another tomorrow to take care of important matters.

God knows our tendency to waste away our days in just a minute here—an hour there. So He asked us to follow the example of His Son who came and lived under the schoolmaster of this world's frustrations, urgencies and time limitations.

As early as the age of twelve, Jesus understood the value of time. After the Feast of Passover. He stayed behind in Jerusalem while his family and friends, unaware, set out for home. When His worried parents returned and finally found Him in the temple, He seemed surprised that they didn't understand why He had to be there:

> Why were you searching for me? he asked. Didn't you know I had to be in my Father's house? But they did not understand what he was saying to them (Luke 2:49–50).

One thing He was saying to them, was that He had no time to waste. He knew that to obey God meant giving every moment of His life to His Father's service, for the moments of this life are limited.

At one point in His ministry He declared to those around Him:

> As long as it is day, we must do the work of him who sent me. Night is coming, when no one can work (John 9:4).

When we run out of time, we run out of opportunities.

Throughout His days on this earth, Jesus demonstrated and taught the importance of loving and serving God with all our heart, soul, mind and time. When a teacher of the law asked Jesus to name the most important commandment, He said:

> Love the Lord your God with all your heart and with all your soul and with all your mind and with all your strength. The second is this: Love your neighbor as yourself. There is go greater commandment than these (Mark 12:30–31).

Jesus clearly understood that we cannot observe these greatest of all commandments to love God wholeheartedly, and love our neighbor selflessly, without spending all of our time at it. For when He said to do this 'with all your strength,' He knew that strength is spent in moments, and that moments are the fabric of our lives.

In the Jewish culture, the funeral service was an important opportunity to show respect for the departed family member. But in Matthew 8:21–22, Jesus revealed a higher priority:

> Another of his disciples said unto him, Lord, suffer me first to go and bury my father. But Jesus said unto him, Follow me; and let the dead bury their dead (KJV).

I'm convinced that God has given us enough time to complete His plan for our life, but not enough time to squander. God has allotted each of us an appointed number of hours for our lives. Our choices become important as they determine how we spend each moment. If we fail to grasp that truth, our lives will be a continual stream of lost minutes, hours and days.

We aren't foolish enough to go over to the trash can and toss in a day or two. We don't literally drop a couple of hours in the toilet and flush. But amusing ourselves takes time. And while God certainly has nothing against rest and renewal, He does vigorously object to frivolous and meaningless squandering of His precious gift of time. He made that abundantly clear to me!

I was also being brought to the understanding that, even good and healthy relaxation in excess, is wasteful. Many things we elect to do may not be wrong in themselves, but God gives us the opportunity to make higher choices. Paul put it this way in I Corinthians 6:12:

> Everything is permissible for me—but not everything is beneficial. Everything is permissible for me—but I will not be mastered by anything.

Paul did not want to spend his time in any way that might cause him to be ensnared by God's second best!

Recently, during a series of meetings in several churches and in several communities, I became extremely tired. I had been able to get only a little sleep, and had been speaking several hours each day. During an afternoon break I was sitting in a motel room wondering if I should sleep, take a walk, read my Bible or pray. But I felt too exhausted to even decide what I should do.

On the end table I saw an attractive looking magazine and reached for it, thinking that might help me to relax. But an unusual question formed in my mind: Could you use this time more profitably if it was your last hour on earth? I had just enough energy left to acknowledge that this was an important thought.

I laid my head back on the chair and prayed, 'Lord, what would you want me to do if this were my last time to talk with you while I'm on earth?'

The Spirit began to minister to me in an unusual way. He helped me to see that hour as a time when He wanted to bless me. If I had missed that opportunity, I would probably have gone through the rest of the day feeling exhausted. But as I listened to the Spirit, I felt all the tiredness being drained out of me. He convinced me that He treasures time spent with us, and that we should consider each moment of life as valuable. That is true wisdom.

> Teach us to number our days aright, that we may gain a heart of wisdom (Psalm 90:12).

12

Balanced Living

I urge you to live a life worthy of the calling you have received (Ephesians 4:1).

The television was turned off, my treasured novels had been replaced with more uplifting reading, and I was doing everything I knew to win one more person to Christ. Had I now arrived? Far from it. It seems there is always more to learn!

One day I woke up knowing that I needed a change of pace. I realized that if I didn't give my body some rest and renewal it would give me plenty of time to reconsider—while I recuperated.

Well, what better way to rest than to go out in the fresh air and play golf? So I dusted off my golf clubs, put them in my car and prepared to go.

'Merlin, what are you doing?'

'Lord, this time I'm doing something good. I'm going to enjoy the beautiful golf course, walk on the green grass in the sunshine, get some needed exercise and rest my mind. This is something I know You approve of.'

'Be sure that you are doing it for My glory.'

That stumped me. Wouldn't I be playing golf for God's glory if I were simply taking care of the health of God's servant? After all, God expects us to be good stewards of all that He entrusts to us, and certainly we are responsible for the care of our bodies!

Perhaps He wanted to free me to rejoice in the fact that I am bringing glory to Him when I take care of my

need for rest. But could He also be wanting me to go
beyond that to discover some deeper truth?

I needed to look at how Jesus rested. Obviously He
slept. Once He was so tired that He fell asleep in a boat
tossed by such a violent storm that His disciples feared
for their lives. Now that's exhaustion! He also found
renewal in solitude as He communed with His Father—
sometimes all night.

But at other times, after teaching and healing and
serving the needs of the crowds, He withdrew with His
close friends and walked and talked, ate, laughed and
shared with them. Maybe that's what the Lord wanted
me to see . . . the special kind of rest found in
relationships!

There might be a discouraged, weary or wounded
believer in need of a brother to play a round of golf with
him and listen to his struggles. Or maybe God knew I
would benefit by sharing my own growing pains and
joys, and so receive understanding and prayer support.
At every tee we could tell one another how glad we are
to know Jesus as Savior, and rejoice together at His
faithful work in our lives. We might even stop to pray,
asking God to help us to be victorious. Now that's the
way to play golf!

Or I could get an unbeliever to play with me, and
spend the entire eighteen holes letting him see how a
Christian enjoys life. We golfers know we need a little
help to have a good game, so I'll start with prayer at the
first tee.

Then I could see myself standing up to the tee and
swinging. My ball sails out-of-bounds in a beautiful slice.
Joy bubbles up and I roar with laughter.

'What are you so happy about?' asks the puzzled
unbeliever. 'Oh, I've learned to be happy about everything, and I couldn't help remembering how unhappy
I used to be before I learned to play golf for God's glory.'

All the way to the next hole I explain the joy of praising

the Lord. On the next tee I decide I should settle down and show my friend that I really do know how to play the game. This time my club misses the ball entirely!

The unbeliever looks at me and watches to see what will happen now. As I look into the sky I say, 'Lord, what a beautiful day this is. Here I am, able to walk around on this wonderful course. I'm healthy, happy and free. Praise You Lord.'

The unbeliever is stuck with me for the entire game. By the last hole he either wishes he had never met me, or he has decided that I have something he needs.

Male or female, young or old, we can, should, and must dedicate every moment of every day, whatever we may be doing—work or rest—to God's glory.

Women can have a great time shopping, as long as they are sure it is for God's reasons. Today's malls are full of lost and lonely people seeking to fill their emptiness with an accumulation of things. As we pray for the people we see, we can take every opportunity to share God's love with them and with the clerks who help us. If we ask God to direct our purchases, our vision, and our conversation, we can go home feeling as if we have been to church.

We can chat on the phone, or get together for coffee or a meal with friends and talk for hours—but only if our central purpose is to please God. A great deal of ministry, both to believers and unbelievers, can happen as we relax together and build relationships for God's glory.

I often challenge people to open their local telephone book and use any available time to call everyone listed.

'Hello, this is Mary Smith. I'm taking a local survey to find out how many people expect to go to heaven. Would you care to comment?'

If they respond favorably by saying, 'Yes, I'm going to heaven,' try to learn if they understand the simple plan of salvation by faith in Jesus.

If they say, 'No, I'm not going to heaven,' ask if they would like you to explain God's gift of eternal life.

One lady accepted my challenge and is now using her telephone to lead an average of one person to Christ each day! When she has additional time she follows up by trying to get each new convert established in a good church. She now wants to continue this work for the rest of her life and is organizing other people in her church to do the same ministry. The financial costs for this project? Nothing! What an opportunity for anyone who has access to a telephone! What a mission field! In your community you may not find one person who has ever received a telephone call, from anyone, inviting them to accept Christ. Calls urging them to buy something? Oh yes, many. The world has great zeal to make money. Let us have great zeal for Christ!

There are games to be played and enjoyed—as long as Jesus is welcome to be there with us! Families need to play together. Shared laughter and fun gives us an opportunity to talk about God's goodness, and teach our children and grandchildren, by example, how to joyfully live out God's Word and His will for our lives. It's important to strengthen the bonds between us and make every minute count so that we will have no regrets regarding how we have spent our time.

I was certainly seeking to do this. And by now I thought I'd pretty much gotten everything centered in God's glory. Then one day I was driving to work when I once again heard that familiar question,

'Merlin, what are you doing?'

'Lord, I'm on my way to the office to do what I can to bring people to know You.'

Apparently He wasn't interested in what I was going to do. He wanted to know what I was doing right then, for He persisted by asking,

'What are you listening to?'

I was listening to the news. My car radio was always

tuned to news or music. It helped to pass the time while I was driving. Was it a waste of time? Turning off the radio, I listened to the unaccustomed silence and began to wonder what I should be doing while driving.

As I meditated, the thought came to me, It's important to be informed about what's going on in this world. But instead of spending all that time listening to other people's opinions and viewpoints, or in being entertained, why not do something more profitable?

I began to wonder if I was becoming too fanatical about everything I did. Perhaps so, but I needed God's answer to that. The best place to find His answers is in His Word, so later that day I searched the Scriptures. My attention was directed to Psalm 37:7:

Be still before the Lord and wait patiently for him.

And again in Psalm 46:10:

Be still, and know that I am God.

The radio wasn't a good place to find silence! What an age we live in! We have words or music flowing into our ears nearly every minute of the day. We can't even go into a store or an elevator, or be put on hold on the phone without being bombarded with sounds. When do we have time to be still and know God's presence? God wanted me to see that we seldom hear His voice until we learn to be quiet.

Life is filled with questions. What should I do about this or that? Wouldn't it be wonderful to be able to hear God's perspective on all these matters?

One day I was driving home after a long day at our Foundation of Praise office. Every minute of the day had been hectic. Whatever could go wrong, did. Now I felt like crawling into a hole and sleeping for a week.

'Merlin, why is your radio on?'

'Oh, sorry. I didn't realize it was on.'

Immediately after flipping the knob off, I saw a young man walking along the street. Some infirmity had so weakened his muscles that he could barely move one foot in front of the other. The Spirit spoke to me,

'Would you prefer to have had your day, or his?'

That got my attention.

If I had listened to the radio instead of to the Lord, I would have gone home too exhausted to do anything worthwhile the entire evening. But the sight of that young man and the question that I heard, changed my focus, filling me with gratitude for my blessings. My day was transformed. I walked into my home with good legs, good health and a heart full of thanksgiving!

Since then, I've learned to listen to the radio only sparingly. My time is too valuable. There is so much that I need to understand and so much that God wants to teach me. I'm learning that travel time can be a very productive time of day—a quiet time to fellowship with Him. There is no hurry, even in a traffic jam, for since He is with me my time is well spent!

I'm often asked, 'How do I learn to hear God speak?' Or, 'How will I know when God is speaking to me?' Or, 'Does He speak in an audible voice?'

God speaks in a still small voice. Our spirit needs silence to learn to listen and recognize His voice. I believe He is continuously speaking words of encouragement, guidance and correction to us—if we will only listen!

Learning takes time and, above all, a strong desire to hear Him. When our attention is on commentators, music and entertainment, we drown Him out.

The 'entertained' mind goes into confusion when there is silence. It could possibly take months for an overly stimulated mind to hear the 'still small voice.' But learning to listen is worth our time and effort, for a true disciple of Jesus has nothing better to do than to listen for the Master's voice.

He calls out to those of us who doze in apathy. He waits to bring new life and joy, and teach us His loving ways. He whispers to us that as we listen and grow, He can help us to live a life of joy and balance in a very unbalanced world.

13

How To Say 'No' And 'Yes'

Clothe yourselves with the Lord Jesus Christ; do not make provision for the flesh to gratify its cravings (Romans 13:14 ML).

The flesh—our human nature, tainted by sin—behaves like a spoiled demanding child. It clamors for the things of this world that will bring pleasure, excitement, stimulation, comfort and ease. It wants them without delay, and without interruption.

Frantically it seeks to feed our five senses, ignoring the needs of the spirit. What looks good? What sounds good? What would taste good, or feel good? The flesh is always sniffing around for something to satisfy its cravings. And the more we feed it, the more it orders us around.

At the time I retired, I told myself that I had earned the right to be entertained, pampered and rewarded. Without realizing what I was doing, I had fanned the desires of the flesh and dampened the fire of the Spirit. God found me laid back and lukewarm. He was not pleased.

Revelation 3:15–16: I know your deeds, that you are neither cold nor hot. I wish you were either one or the other! So, because you are lukewarm—neither hot nor cold—I am about to spit you out of my mouth.

I had to repent, and then learn how to say 'no' to myself, and 'yes' to God's Spirit.

Denying the clamoring desires of the flesh is not easy,

I can tell you! So if you are one who has decided that your flesh has been in charge long enough, you will need to practice speaking firmly to yourself. (Why not talk to yourself? The world already thinks we Christians are crazy!) But be prepared for the flesh to argue and fight every step of the way.

When you rise early in the morning for prayer, your flesh will groan, 'What good is this?'

Say to it, 'Flesh, this means that you are not in control of my life. My spirit is getting up to fellowship with God. Be quiet!'

When you kneel to pray the flesh will undoubtedly suggest, 'Why not pray in bed? That would be easier, warmer and far better for your back!'

'I know what you're up to,' you will say, 'you want me to go to sleep!'

When you follow Jesus' recommendation to fast and pray, the flesh will object, 'What are you trying to do, kill yourself?'

'Be quiet. People kill themselves from overeating, not with fasting and prayer. You have led me away from God many times, but now the Holy Spirit is leading me to obey Jesus.'

One way to grow stronger in our commitment to pray, is to learn to be 'entertained'—captured with delight, absorbed, fascinated!—by conversing with God.

In the beginning there's a good chance you will feel more bored and tired than fascinated. Expect the flesh to declare your efforts a waste of time.

But don't give up, you can learn to enjoy prayer. The flesh is simply rebelling against the spirit. God isn't upset. He is delighted that you are praying! His desire is to help you, if you persevere.

Once you learn to find pleasure in prayer, you will have a new relationship with God. The communication you establish with Him will open new horizons of joy and delight.

But don't expect that to stop the flesh from giving you problems in other areas. Suppose you are watching a TV program, and feel that God wants you to turn it off. The flesh will argue, 'There's nothing wrong with watching this. This is the way the real world is! Are you afraid of real life?'

Try quoting Scripture to your flesh:

> Real life is in Jesus Who said, I have come that they may have life, and have it to the full (John 10:10).

'I am going to use this time to pray for people who are caught up in this kind of empty life—people who need to discover life to the full in Christ!'

The more difficult it is for us to turn off that show, deny ourselves a meal, get out of bed or do anything the flesh doesn't like, the greater opportunity we have to become stronger in spirit!

There is an important difference between having a strong spirit, and a willing spirit. Weak Christians often display a willing spirit. This willing spirit combined with their weak flesh says, 'I would get out of bed now if I weren't so tired.' Or, 'I would give up this bad habit if it weren't so difficult for me.' Or, 'I would study God's Word if I had more time, or if I understood it better.'

The strong spirit says, 'There is a need for action so I am going to do it. It will be hard, for I have become addicted to pleasing my flesh, but I will do it in God's strength.'

I had certainly become addicted to amusing myself with television, movies and other entertainment. When our evening meal was over my first thought was always, What's on TV tonight? We are told that a habit can be broken in 30 days. But for me it took much longer. While relaxing in front of the television screen will probably always be a temptation, it no longer has first place in my thoughts.

A habit is a mental attitude or a behavior acquired by practice. Because such attitudes or actions are ingrained by repetition, they have a deep and subtle influence on us. Habitual responses are no longer a part of our conscious thought pattern or choices. They have moved into the realm of subconscious prodding.

With the conscious mind we might think, I want a glass of cold water. And then we pick it up with our right hand, not because we stood there debating about which hand to use, but because we have already acquired the habit that tells the brain which hand to use. Habit dictates.

If we have fallen into the habit of indulging the flesh in some way, we will need to become aware of it and confess it to God. Such confession brings our habit up to the conscious mind where decisions are made. Over and over we will be required to choose against what has almost become instinct to us. It will be a struggle, but we will develop a strong spirit through such exercise, and we will eventually be free.

As we give up the things of the flesh, we make room for the things of the Spirit. God gave us His Holy Spirit as a gift. Each time we deny our flesh what it wants, we give His Spirit a little more of us! The more He has of us, the more we will notice His calm, gentle Spirit working in our hearts and minds. His strength will fill us in new ways, making us fruitful:

> Be delighted (entertained) with the Lord. Then He will give you all your heart's desires (Psalm 37:4).

Remember the beautiful plane I bought myself so that I could indulge my love of flying? Well I finally sold that plane, because I believed it was holding me back from walking in the Spirit. As soon as I did, a new strength flowed into my spirit. The flow was so strong I felt it!

There wasn't anything wrong with having a plane.

The problem was it kept me from fulfilling God's purpose for my life. Nothing must be allowed to do that.

Jesus warned us about this problem when He said:

> The desires for other things come in and choke the word, making it unfruitful (Mark 4:19).

What are those 'other things?' They are anything that prevents us from doing our best to complete God's plan for our lives.

Jesus said:

> The seed that fell among thorns stands for those who hear, but as they go on their way they are choked by life's worries, riches and pleasures, and they do not mature (Luke 8:14).

Has the seed of eternal life been sown in you? Is it growing, or wilting from self indulgence?

We will know we are 'lukewarm' Christians if we become so busy with our own problems, pleasures and pursuits we fail to take God's Good News to hurting people.

Once we realize what has happened to us we can center our attention on Jesus' words:

> I seek not to please myself but him who sent me (John 5:30).

We can learn to follow His example! It's not going to be easy for any of us. We will have to give up things our human nature desperately wants to keep, but we can do it.

I Samuel 10:6 tells us:

> The Spirit of the Lord will come upon you in power . . . and you will be changed into a different person.

In Christ, and through the Holy Spirit's work in our life, we who are obedient are actually becoming a 'different person.'

How can we be ready for the changes that will come as His Spirit fills us? If you are being changed in this way, it's important to stop thinking of yourself as the same person you have been most of your life. Be new in Christ—in the way you think and feel about yourself. With the help of the Holy Spirit there is nothing you can't accomplish for Him.

Say with the apostle Paul:

> One thing I do: Forgetting what is behind and straining toward what is ahead, I press on toward the goal (Philippians 3:13–14).

Forget the good or the bad you have done. Rejoice in His presence and let Him work in you now.

Jesus wants to have close fellowship with men and women who want to be like Him. Each time we deny our flesh and submit to His will, we become stronger in spirit and a litte more like Christ. He transforms us into His image, and we become His ambassadors:

> We are therefore Christ's ambassadors, as though God were making his appeal through us (II Corinthians 5:20).

An ambassador is an envoy of the highest rank who is sent to a foreign country. But we are not sent to serve without pay:

> Behold, I am coming soon! My reward is with me, Jesus says, and I will give to everyone according to what he has done (Revelation 22:12).

Every moment we give in service to God will be rewarded! He offers eternal benefits based upon our faithful obedience to His Son. He even releases some of His rewards while we are still on earth!

Jesus said:

> All that belongs to the Father is mine. That is why I said the Spirit will take from what is mine and make it known to you (John 16:15).

The Spirit gives to us what belongs to Christ. What an amazing truth! When we understand this, nothing in this book seems burdensome.

> Therefore, stand firm. Let nothing move you. Always give yourselves fully to the work of the Lord, because you know that your labor in the Lord is not in vain (I Corinthians 15:58).

14

Get Back Into The Race!

Let us throw off everything that hinders and the sin that so easily entangles, and let us run with perseverance the race marked out for us (Hebrews 12:1).

You have entered the race. But perhaps you've been tripped up, or slowed down by this world's attractive entanglements. I found myself entangled in the desire to be constantly entertained. I was hindered by the comfort of retirement and rest. I was weighted down with things designed to enhance my enjoyment of life. God woke me up.

If the experiences I have shared in this book have served as a wake up call to you, I praise God! And I want to offer all the help possible to get you back into the race.

In the following chapters, you will find thoughts on several seductive hazards that have the power to sidetrack and render us ineffective. Many of us are weak because we have allowed ourselves to prefer such pleasures or pursuits over loving God.

As the Holy Spirit leads us to terminate our involvement with those entertainments that are causing us problems, we may think, 'This is miserable. Why can't I be like an ordinary Christian and have some fun?'

How soon we get over withdrawal pains will depend on:

1. How long we have been addicted.
2. How determined we are to be free.

   3. How quickly we learn that God's entertainment is more satisfying than anything Satan has contrived.

At the end of each chapter dealing with a particular hindrance you will find a list of pertinent Scriptures. Study these carefully, and meditate on them, letting them sink deep into your heart. For it is not man's words, but God's Word that has the power to set us free.

There is something else that will be very helpful to you. As you read prayerfully through the following chapters, ask the Lord to shine His light on any problem areas He sees. Develop a plan for change. Your future will hold nothing superior to your past unless you make changes. It's going to take some thinking—perhaps real concentration.

Many Christians have never made the effort to learn who they are and what they want to be. Have you ever told God what you intend to do with your life? If not, now is your opportunity.

Select which prayer you want to make:

   1. God, I want to have fun most of my life and serve You with whatever time I have left over.
   2. Father, I want to serve You the rest of my life and trust You to give me the fun and happiness that is best for me.

If the real truth is that you prefer to serve the Lord when it is convenient, then admit it. Be honest enough with yourself, and with God, to draw a line and say, 'This is what I want.' But make that line clear so that you will know where you are. Our flesh always wants to avoid taking a clear cut position with God, as though we can somehow keep the truth from Him. But He already knows. It is we who need to know the truth.

Take out a pencil and write here in this book or on a piece of paper, 'The following are the ways I use any free time that life has allotted to me:'

1.

2.

3.

Now do something that our flesh usually deplores. Add up the average time you spend each day in doing those activities. Include time spent in reading the newspaper, listening to the news, talking with family or friends on the telephone, etc. How does that time compare with the opportunities you take to fellowship with God?

And then say, 'Lord, I intend to keep on doing these things,' or else say, 'Father, I'm not pleased with all that I have been doing and this is what I plan to do instead':

1.

2.

3.

If you realize that you have not been spending your time in ways that are pleasing to God, then wage a battle to change your life. You have just written a new set of goals. Find ways to live them out!

At first you may be able to modify only one segment of each day. During that particular time, sing praises to God. Don't allow yourself to think one unhappy thought. Be really glad that you are a child of God and are on your way to heaven. When you feel truly glad, plot some strategy to share your joy with someone else.

You will reach the point where you can ask yourself, 'How many people will hear the Good News of the Gospel because I have been forgiven of my sins?' Then you can decide just how much passion, zeal and determination you will have to tell people what God has done for you.

Plan your desired objective! Don't concern yourself at this point with how you are going to do it. Just decide that your unchangeable reason for living will be to find ways to bring others to Christ and to strengthen His children.

Now it is time to set about seeking new ways to introduce others to Christ. Don't let your intentions be some vague concept in your mind. God wrote out His Words to you, so why not write out words to Him? Put your plans and objectives on paper where you can see them. The Holy Spirit is here on earth to assist anyone who wants to tell others the Good News about Jesus. He will bless and use anyone who has a clear-cut goal to do God's will.

When you write your objectives don't simply say, 'I'll serve God all of my life.' Decide specifically what you will do. How will you serve? Decide when you will serve. Decide how much time of this day will be spent toward accomplishing a particular goal.

For every goal ask, and answer: 'what,' 'how,' 'who,' 'when,' and 'where?'

The following are a few sample questions and possible answers:

What is my goal? (To prepare my mind and heart to serve God.)

How do I do that? (Through studying God's Word and in prayer.)

Who can help me accomplish this? (I will ask the Holy Spirit to interpret the Scriptures to my heart, and to help me as I pray; and I will also join a Bible study course or prayer group with Christian friends.)

When will I do this? (I will get up one hour earlier each morning to study God's Word and pray. The Bible study course or prayer group meets on Wednesday evenings at 7:00. I am writing that on my calendar.)

Where will I accomplish this? (I will go to my desk to read the Bible and pray, so that I won't be tempted to crawl back into bed.)

If you run into difficulty following through with a goal or an objective, you can problem solve by asking the same series of questions.

What is interfering with my carrying out my plan to study God's Word and pray for an hour every morning? (I am just too tired to get up every morning.) What can I do to solve that problem? (I will go to bed one hour earlier each night so that I won't be so tired.) And then work through the what-how-who-when-where plan to make certain you will actually do that.

Or maybe you might decide that studying and praying at a different time of day would be more productive. In that case you would ask and answer the series of questions to bring that new goal to life.

This is a plan of action that God can bless. This is an approach that cooperates fully with God as He brings about changes in your life that are needed. Determine to take these goals with you into the obstacle course ahead. God will help you every step of the way. He will not be displeased if you, like the Prodigal Son, are moving in the right direction.

As you persevere, God will cut you free of the entanglements of this world. Then you can get on with the race to win the glorious prize for which God has called us heavenward!

15

Lured By Electronic Entertainment

Turn my eyes away from worthless things (Psalm 119:37).

Recently the *New Yorker* reported that more American homes have televisions than have indoor plumbing. And in the average home, that television is on about seven hours a day. One in every eight adults admitted to being addicted to television.

Millions of us, in order to expand our choices and access Hollywood's latest offerings, have also purchased VCR machines. Then, so that we can operate these entertainment systems without moving from our easy chairs, we get remote control devices.

The music industry offers us a variety of ways to saturate our minds with their rhythms and lyrics. They have us replacing our record albums with cassette tapes, compact discs, and music videos. For those who have any time left, there are computer games. Some children refuse to visit a relative without their Nintendo game in tow. There seems to be no end to the options for entertainment offered by our electronic age.

The word entertainment means, 'to hold the attention of, to amuse, to agreeably divert.' It comes from the Latin word meaning 'to hold between.'

No wonder the world uses its growing electronic capabilities to produce entertainment of every sort with such determination. Where there is no hope, a diversion is not only welcome, it is desperately needed. The search never ends for some amusing thing 'to hold between' them and their emptiness.

We Christians have within us a Living Hope, yet we get caught up in the multitude of the world's amusements. Their movies, TV shows, music and electronic games cleverly occupy our attention and manage to 'divert' us from our commission to share the Good News of Christ with that lost and dying world. These entertainments become substitute pleasures for the delight that we would be finding in God's presence and with His people . . . and thus the enemy 'holds them between' us and our Lord.

But our feasting at the world's smorgasbord of entertainment holds more hazards than just diverting us from our task and from fellowship with God. They contaminate us.

Senator Robert Byrd was quoted as saying, 'On most given nights, with a flick of a remote control device, the living rooms of average American families can be treated to a melange of foul-mouthed brats uttering language for which any stranger entering those same living rooms and uttering that same language would probably be immediately thrown out bodily, and the use of which in any polite company would earn its user a reputation as a boor and a lout.'

But it is worse, even, than that. In an article called, *When God Departs!* (11/91), David Wilkerson says, 'In millions of Christian homes, so-called normal, godly people sit before cable TV or a VCR and drink in filthy, shameful R- and X-rated movies! . . . TV networks and cable companies now compete to bring the vilest, most perverted movies into America's homes. And untold numbers of 'believing Christians' now secretly view this filth! . . . If it has taken hold of you, it will destroy you.'

And we aren't just occasionally watching television. One poll concluded adults spend 40 percent of their lesiure time watching TV. This places television viewing third, just behind sleep and work in weekly hours spent by adults. And according to a survey by Dr. Ted Baehr, Christians are watching the same amount of R-rated movies as non-Christians!

Not only are we damaged by the corrupt content of what we view, but God will surely call His children to account for trafficking with the depraved industry that produces this trash. Few people could have more first hand knowledge of what really goes on in this industry than actress, Gloria Swanson did.

Gloria was a glamorous movie star back in the thirties, and was still well known in the seventies. She came to Escondido, California and met with me. She had read *Prison to Praise*, and wanted to know how to receive Jesus as her personal Savior. She listened intently as I explained the Good News of the Gospel. When she understood, she received Jesus as her Savior, and then came forward in our Sunday morning church service to make her decision public.

Gloria worked in Hollywood for fifty years. She described it as 'a cesspool'. 'It destroys eveyone in it. Young, talented girls are forced to satisfy every lust and passion of those who control the huge sums of money that are involved. Beautiful young girls and boys have to sacrifice themselves on the altar of sex or they never get ahead in movies.' Gloria was bitter and angry over the god of entertainment.

Some of you remember the loveable character, Dennis the Menace, on television shows in the early 60's. What could be more innocent? Yet Jay North, who played the character Dennis, has sordid memories. Recently on NBC news Jay said, 'It's an evil, vile system. I hated every minute of it. They made my life a living hell for four years. I was terrified of everyone. The people who run TV are cruel. They don't care about anybody except making money. Show business destroys people.'

In her autobiography Shirley Temple says they

demanded that she play the character, Shirley Temple, to perfection. If she didn't, they put her in a box too small to stand up in, with a block of ice!

In the *USA Weekend*, March 29, 1992, movie critic Michael Medved says: 'In the remake of the film *Cape Fear*, America's most acclaimed director, Martin Scorsese, created an utterly gratuitous scene in which De Niro, one of our most distinguished actors, bites off the cheek of his victim in the midst of sex, then . . .' (The remainder of the quote is so gruesome that I will not include it.) Mr. De Niro's Hollywood peers nominated his performance as a favorite for a 1992 Oscar nomination!

While our association with this industry is damaging us, it is literally destroying our children. They are being 'educated' by television and movies. Violence, sexual distortions and disrespect are normal, everyday experiences. President Bush said that he is convinced TV's excesses are having a bad effect on our children, their ability to learn, and family stability. His message to parents: 'Don't make the mistake of thinking your kids learn only from 9 a.m. to 3 p.m.'

Ian Mitroff, co-author of *The Unreality Industry*, says that television damages our brains in two ways. First, it electronically manufactures unreality in such a way that we can't distinguish it from the real. Then it makes those distortions so entertaining that we no longer even care what is real and what isn't.

The magazine *Insight*, in the July 1, 1991 issue, says '*Prime Time World* is the "church" where the average American worships about four hours daily, absorbing Hollywood's secular sermonizing. The preaching comes from pulpits disguised as sitcoms, cop shows and made-for-TV movies.'

We must wake up and care! As Christians, we are required to distinguish between the real (the Kingdom of God), and the unreal (the twisted and temporary

pleasures of the kingdom of this world.) Time is short.
This is what the Lord is saying to us:

> Do not share in the sins of others. Keep yourself pure (I
> Timothy 5:22).

> But I am afraid that just as Eve was deceived by the
> serpent's cunning, your minds may somehow be led astray
> from your sincere and pure devotion to Christ (II Corinthians
> 11:3).

> Don't copy the behavior and customs of this world . . .
> Then you will learn from your own experience how His ways
> will really satisfy you (Romans 12:2 TLB).

> If those who have escaped the contaminations of the world
> through the knowledge of our Lord and Savior Jesus Christ,
> are again entangled and overcome by them, then their last
> condition becomes worse than the first (II Peter 2:20 ML).

> Ye shall not go after other gods, the gods of the people
> which are round about you (Deuteronomy 6:14 KJV).

> Blessed is the man who does not walk in the counsel of
> the wicked, or stand in the way of sinners, or sit in the seat
> of mockers (Psalm 1:1 KJV).

> All will be condemned who have not believed the truth
> but have delighted in wickedness (II Thessalonians 2:12).

> Be holy now in everything you do, just as the Lord is holy,
> who invited you to be His child. He Himself has said, You
> must be holy, for I am holy (I Peter 1:15–16 TLB).

16

Hooked On Sports And Fitness

You were running a good race. Who cut in on you and kept you from obeying the truth? (Galatians 5:7).

I have always loved sports. As a young man I often ran the mile to our old deserted-lot playing field so I could play football, baseball or basketball. In college I was on the baseball team. As a private in the Army I was selected to play basketball for our regiment.

Participating in sports can be a healthy form of exercise, and a wonderful way to build friendships. Spectator sports offer less benefits but are an enjoyable experience for many people.

The big problem is the precious time they take. Sports can become consuming. It is painful for me to admit, but when I was retired I sometimes watched two football games in a day. What used to be just Monday night football, has stretched to one or more televised sports events nearly every day of the week, placing constant temptation before sports fans.

Football and baseball once built strength and character into their participants. But the move from vacant lots and school campuses into huge stadiums that seat over 100,000 people, has changed them from a sport to an entertainment event. These games are big time entertainment, featuring superstars who draw big time salaries. What a waste of valuable time and resources!

Even sports such as wrestling, boxing, tennis and soccer, now draw unbelievably enormous crowds of spectators—plus the millions who watch on television. Golf tournaments that were at one time quiet, dignified affairs can now have as many as 20,000 people gathered about one hole to see if the golf ball will go into it!

I'm not saying that it's wrong to watch sports. I have friends who invite relatives and acquaintances to gather in their home for some sporting events. They supply food and a happy atmosphere. They also find creative ways to make it an occasion to honor God.

Sometimes they have researched the Christian testimony of one of the players. After reading their testimony, they ask everyone to join in prayer that God will use the player to win others to Christ. This opens the door to conversation about the joyful difference we see in the lives of athletes who put Jesus first, over those who seek only money, popularity and the fast life.

When I occasionally watch a special sporting event, I'm always compelled by the Spirit to pray for any Christians involved, asking God to help them serve Him. Many born again athletes are having a tremendous impact on young people, as they take a public stand for Christ.

Sometimes these same youngsters have a Christian father whose actions demonstrate that they love sports more than they love their own family. Such men will spend three hours watching sports, or playing golf or some other game, and in the same day fail to spend three minutes in strengthening the spiritual life of their children.

Then there are those families who are so involved with children's sports that their entire lives revolve around practices, games and tournaments. These parents and their children are often unable to attend Bible studies or worship services, or enter into ministry efforts because the games claim first priority. Some churches even feel compelled to plan their schedule so they don't interfere with members who have games to watch or attend. And that means sports have cut in on the real race we are called to run.

Closely related to sports is the matter of physical fitness. When a Believer exercises and takes good care of his body, he or she honors God. We are the temple of His Holy Spirit. So when we care for our body, we care for God's dwelling place.

It is a sad truth, however, that our enemy tries to turn any good effort into a false god by encouraging us to get out of balance—by getting us to place a higher priority on that thing than on God Himself.

The worthy goal of being fit can all too easily escalate into a passion. Some people become addicted to running or working out, devoting huge amounts of time to the effort. Certain muscle groups must be built up. Then we need another exercise machine because other muscles need more attention to be well balanced. Special diets are undertaken. Lavishing this much attention on the body is a form of idolatry.

Do we even notice when we cross the line from concern about fitness to concern about body image? An impressive physique impresses. We live in a nation that places a very high priority on beautiful bodies. The media and advertisers constantly bombard us with the message that being attractive is sexy and important.

Exercise, sports, fitness and beauty are all subject to the higher goal of spiritual fitness and beauty. God has something to say to those of us who need to focus more on inner strength:

> Spend your time and energy in the exercise of keeping spiritually fit (I Timothy 4:7 TLB).

> Verse 8: Bodily exercise is all right, but spiritual exercise is much more important . . .

> Do you not know that in a race all the runners run, but only one gets the prize? Run in such a way as to get the prize. Everyone who competes in the games goes into strict

training. They do it to get a crown that will not last; but we do it to get a crown that will last forever (I Corinthians 9:24–25).

God has bought you with a great price, So use every part of your body to give glory back to God, because He owns it (I Corinthians 6:20 TLB).

I am coming soon. Hold on to what you have, so that no one will take your crown. Him who overcomes I will make a pillar in the temple of my God. Never again will he leave it. I shall write on him the name of my God (Revelation 3:11–12).

17

Caught In The Earning And Spending Trap

He who loves pleasure will become poor (Proverbs 21:17).

I wonder how many cars driven by Christians, sport that popular bumper sticker: 'Born to Shop!' I wonder how many others would be displaying such a sign if the truth dared to print itself out and somehow attach itself to us.

I can hear some men saying, 'My wife would be wearing a big one of those signs, I can tell you! She's got a whole closet crammed full of clothes, but does that stop her? Either she's gained weight, or lost weight, or else it's out of style, or the color's not right. Always some excuse. I think shopping is her hobby! I'm going broke!'

Yet the men doing the complaining—guys who wouldn't think of wasting money on unnecessary clothes—often sink endless dollars into tools, sporting goods, cars, and computer or electronic equipment, or some hobby or collection.

The world is loaded with things designed to create a hankering in the heart of anyone with a dollar or a credit card. There's always something newer, better, faster, tastier, softer, prettier, different, or upgraded to make what we own undesirable.

And even if we decide not to replace it, it's likely to break down or wear out. Quality in merchandising has given way to built-in obsolescence. So our landfills are loaded with the waste of our cheap gadgetry, our hearts are filled with discontent, and our wallets are empty. More than empty. We spend far more than we earn.

I hear from hundreds of hard working people who are getting deeper and deeper in debt. Deficits cause them ever increasing anxiety. They can think of nothing else. It is possible that some of these people are living frugally and wisely, but their income simply cannot keep pace with even the basic cost of living in this inflated society.

It is far more likely that the vast majority have been trapped into living above their means. Many people choose to live in a high cost area and buy a home so expensive that two incomes are required to stay afloat. That means two cars are needed, increased insurance, nice clothes, furniture to fill the bigger home, and they have to pay someone to care for the children. They work constantly and are tired, stressed and have little time to enjoy one another or the things that their money has bought.

They and their families have bought the message sent out by Madison Avenue, via the enemy: 'You deserve all the nice things you want. You need it. You'll look good, smell good, feel good. Everybody else has it. No money down!' And so they've gotten things that they don't need (and are certain they can't live without) but can not afford. They've allowed their resources to be drained by their desires. They are ashamed and exhausted, but don't know what to do.

It is not this world, or the things of this world that should command our affection and resources. We need to tell ourselves this truth: However attractive, colorful, and desirable the wares of this world, we are not born to shop. We are born again to serve, love and give ourselves away. This requires us to live simple, clean uncluttered lives.

Does this law of simplicity apply only to those who are struggling financially? Even if we can afford to spend our time and money obtaining luxuries, can we afford to spend our lives that way when there is a lost and hurting world at our door?

Besides, there are special pitfalls for the successful businessman, the entrepreneur, and the professional. It is easy to become consumed by a career and the desire to advance or expand. The effort to achieve can be entertaining. There is always the next rung on the ladder to success—whatever the cost. There's another factory to buy, another business to control, another product to acquire, another risky venture to challenge the limits. The passion to possess and control can cost them everything, so that they spend the rest of life (or eternity) in regret.

Some who have been caught up in this frenzy to acquire have said to me, 'Why was I so stupid?'

This kind of driven desire happens for one reason. The tempter has found a weak spot—an area where our desires are not subject to the laws of God—where we are driven by a love for things of this world, rather than the things of God's Kingdom. Whether we are rich, poor, or somewhere in between, if the enemy can keep our appetite for more and better things stirred up, he has us under his influence. He is out to destroy our peace, families, health and our ability to be productive in other areas of our lives.

Jesus leads us in the opposite direction. He teaches us to hunger for righteousness, not things. He advises us to become more like the birds of the air and the flowers of the field, trusting God to supply our needs. He invites us to take time off from feeding the never ending cravings of our flesh, so that we can relax, sing and be truly happy.

Yet billions of dollars are spent in our country in an effort to get these physical bodies groomed and attired in something that might make us look good. There is clothing, jewelry, makeup, hairdressers, manicurists and spas. We are quite intent about all of this. The

messages of the media brainwash us into believing that
if the outside looks fabulous, relationships will be good,
and we will feel good inside. It doesn't work that way.

I am not advocating slovenliness. I believe God wants
us to look as clean, neat and presentable as possible, as
long as we don't get caught up in excessive concern over
our appearance. No one could claim that God is opposed
to beauty—He has lavished color, texture, design and
beauty throughout His creation. And He was the first
tailor!

> The Lord God made garments of skin for Adam and his
> wife and clothed them (Genesis 3:21).

However, God also knows that it is not what is on the
outside, but rather the motives of our heart, and our
priorities and attitudes that can truly make us feel good—
whatever we happen to look like on the outside.

Once when I was scheduled to speak at a large church
the host picked me up at the motel. I slipped into my
suit coat and we headed for the church. When we were
in the pastor's office, I noticed several of the elders
looking at me rather intensely, I thought, 'Hm, what's
the problem?'

We walked down the aisle and up to the platform.
While the pastor was conducting the preliminaries I
happened to look down. During the afternoon I had
gone out for a walk wearing an old pair of trousers. You
guessed it, I still had them on! And they didn't even
come close to matching my suit coat.

This was my opportunity to find out what was more
important to me—my chance to help people, or my
appearance? So when I stepped up to speak, I asked the
congregation how they liked my wardrobe. We all
enjoyed a hearty laugh, and I discovered a wonderful
truth. When the joy of our heart is to serve God, we
don't need to seek approval for how we look. Our
attitude is worth far more than our outfit.

In all of life, it is our attitude toward the things of this world that will judge us as righteous or unrighteous. Do we covet things, seek things, spend excessive amounts of precious time and energy acquiring things? Do our desires lead us into debt? Or, as God entrusts to us the goods of this world, do we hold them in an open hand, quite content if we have them or if we don't?

What does the Lord have to say about all this?

Love not the world, neither the things that are in the world (I John 2:15 KJV).

What good will it be for a man if he gains the whole world, yet forfeits his soul? Or what can a man give in exchange for his soul? (Matthew 16:26).

Why spend money on what is not bread, and your labor on what does not satisfy? Listen to me and eat what is good, and your soul will delight in the richest of fare (Isaiah 55:2).

If you lack the means to pay, your very bed will be snatched from under you (Proverbs 22:27).

Be content with your pay (Luke 3:14).

But godliness with contentment is great gain. For we brought nothing into the world, and we can take nothing out of it. But if we have food and clothing, we will be content with that. People who want to get rich fall into temptation and a trap and into many foolish and harmful desires that plunge men into ruin and destruction. For the love of money is a root of all kinds of evil (I Timothy 6:6–10).

Command those who are rich . . . to be rich in good deeds, and to be generous and willing to share. In this way they will lay up treasure for themselves as a firm foundation for the coming age, so that they may take hold of the life that is truly life (I Timothy 6:17–19).

Honor the Lord with your wealth (Proverbs 3:9).

The blessing of the Lord brings wealth, and he adds no trouble to it (Proverbs 10:22).

18

Weighed Down By Food And Fun

*Their god is their appetite . . . and all they think about is
this life here on earth* (Philippians 3:19 TLB).

Some folks have been conditioned to be unhappy if
they aren't surrounded by people and fun. As far as
they're concerned, silence is not golden. And solitude
is a punishment. Their life's motto is: 'Let's have a party!
Food, fun and frolic!' They'll get together to celebrate
just about anything with anybody. Excursions and
evenings out are constantly in the works. The important
thing is that the excitement and fun keep rolling.

As church members, such people will attend every
meeting and function. And if there aren't enough
programmed activities, they will manage to get something new scheduled—banquets, luncheons, desserts,
or potlucks—if it has food it's even better. If they have
to sit at home for an evening, the church is failing in its
duty to entertain them.

Now I don't deny that some people are, by nature,
extremely outgoing and gregarious, while others are
more introverted and quiet. There's nothing wrong with
that. God created the differences, and He uses us for
different purposes.

But as with any good thing, the problem comes when
we get out of balance. If we're not happy unless we're
socializing constantly, we are in trouble. We are addicted
to people as entertainment.

Or if we're not happy unless we constantly have

something good to eat—if food is our source of pleasure, comfort and satisfaction—we are in trouble.

You may not have been able to relate to, or identify with the entertainments to which other people are addicted, because you have no great interest in any of them. Your entertainment may simply be food—with or without people around. It may be that if you can eat what you want, when you want, and as much as you want, then you can freely deny yourself many other pleasures. To you, a fantastic evening out means going to a great restaurant and indulging yourself.

Many physicians believe that eating too much, as well as eating the wrong things, causes more sickness and death than any other cause. That should get our attention. And it should give us some idea that food is one of the weapons that Satan seeks to use against us to destroy our ability to serve God. He has been at it since the beginning of time.

God had told Adam and Eve that they could eat from any tree in the garden except the one in the middle, for if they ate from that they would die. But with a little help from the serpent, Eve 'saw that the fruit of the tree was good for food and pleasing to the eye, and also desirable . . .' so she ate it. And she no longer had a perfect heart. (Genesis 3)

Esau sold his birthright—a very special blessing from God—for one bowl of food. (Genesis 25)

The Israelites were repeatedly in trouble with God because they wanted different food than what He provided for them. (Exodus 16)

Satan used the promise of food to tempt Jesus when He hadn't eaten for forty days. (Matthew 4)

Jesus told one group of people that they were only interested in Him because they thought He would feed them. (John 6)

Daniel refused the temptation to eat the king's rich food, and chose to eat only vegetables and drink water.

At the end of ten days he looked healthier and better nourished than those who ate the royal food. He was recognized by men and by God, as being an unusually wise man, and he demonstrated his wisdom even in what he ate and drank. (Daniel 1)

What I'm about to say may cause me to lose friends, but I can not ignore any truth that will help God's people to be strong in spirit. We cannot justify being opposed to alcohol, cigarettes or illegal drugs, if we in turn use food in a way that damages our health.

If we have an excessive delight in eating, we can learn how to give the Holy Spirit control of that place in our heart.

When Jesus' disciples were concerned that He didn't take time to eat, He told them that He had food they didn't know anything about. (John 4:32) That verse can be a marvelous key to many people's dilemma. Once we learn to be delighted in the Lord, He begins to feed us in that empty, hungry place that we've been trying to fill with food. He satisfies our desire for entertainment, relaxation and comfort, and He opens our understanding to new joys—joys about which we may never have heard.

Habitual dieters will be delighted to know that it is possible to be set free from bondage regarding food. Victory lies in saturating our heart with everything that will increase our fellowship with God. He offers us prayer, Bible study, opportunities to witness for Him, and times of uniting with other Christians in worship. Once the Holy Spirit is in charge of that area, then He helps us to enjoy food without being dominated by it!

As we enter into communion with God 'with all our heart,' we begin to receive many of the 'desires of our heart.' We learn to feast on the Bread of Life, and drink from the Living Water and be satisfied. And soon 'former things (old out of control appetites and desires) are passed away, and behold, all things have become new!'

God gave us the gifts of food and fellowship so that we would be healthy in body and spirit. We can reclaim these gifts, rescuing them from the enemy's grip, as we learn to follow Jesus' example and enjoy food and fellowship in a balanced way that is pleasing to God and good for us.

Jesus certainly went to celebrations, feasts and parties. His first public miracle was performed at a wedding party.

He enjoyed many relaxed meals with His disciples. As they ate and shared their experiences, He taught them things about the Father and His kingdom, and they grew together in the bond of love.

There is also some indication that Jesus was criticized by the religious leaders for His fellowship with the wrong kind of people. When He entered the homes of the outcasts of society and joined in their feasts, the outraged Pharisees and teachers of the law said:

> This man welcomes sinners and eats with them (Luke 15:2).

Custom held that eating with a person indicated acceptance and recognition. Jesus elevated these rejected people with His presence and love, showing us that it is possible to use times of food and fellowship to make an eternal difference in the lives of others.

The Lord has Words of wisdom to help us:

> The kingdom of God is not a matter of eating and drinking, but of righteousness, peace and joy in the Holy Spirit (Romans 14:17–18).

> Do not work for food that spoils, but for food that endures to eternal life, which the Son of Man will give you (John 6:27).

> Dearly beloved, I beseech you as strangers and pilgrims, abstain from fleshly lusts, which war against the soul (I Peter 2:11).

So I say, live by the Spirit and you will not gratify the desires of the sinful nature (Galatians 5:16).

My food, said Jesus, is to do the will of him who sent me and to finish his work (John 4:34).

I am the living bread that came down from heaven. If anyone eats of this bread, he will live forever (John 6:51).

Blessed are those who hunger and thirst for righteousness, for they will be filled (Matthew 5:6).

19

Sidetracked By Retirement

You . . . keep your covenant of love with your servants who continue wholeheartedly in your way (II Chronicles 6:14).

It's hard to believe, but God does not seem to have a retirement plan for His workers! I have been unable to find retirement, either the word or the concept, anywhere in the New Testament. It seems to be a modern, not a Christian, concept.

Today we figure it this way: you work hard all your life, and then at a certain age you get to settle back to rest and play, reaping the rewards of all that hard work.

So we find an easy chair to watch TV and listen to music. We read. We potter around the house and garden. We enjoy a hobby, or collection. We visit with friends and family. We play golf or other non-stressful games. We eat out. We go shopping. We get motor homes and travel around the country. We go to church once in a while—or maybe even regularly.

But most of us don't work too hard at church. After all, we've done our stint there. It's up to the young folk now. We'll just sit back and enjoy the fellowship, music and preaching of the Word. We don't mind giving a suggestion now and then. But that's about it, because we're retired.

Once in a while, however, we find someone in our ranks who is an elder, or still serves on the deacon board, or teaches a class, or heads up the missions committee, or disciples new Christians, or works with troubled youth, or goes calling on shut-ins. We figure it's nice of them to continue to serve when they don't really have to—nice of them to be willing to share their years of wisdom. They're probably the type who would be bored if they weren't doing something, if they didn't have their finger in the pie somewhere.

And we don't realize that they aren't being nice, or overcoming boredom. They are simply being obedient disciples of Christ! As long as it is day, we hear Jesus remind us, we must do the work of him who sent Me (John 9:4). Do you still have some daylight left?

> The important thing to remember is that our remaining time is very short, and so are our opportunities for doing the Lord's work . . . happiness or sadness or wealth (or retirement) should not keep anyone from doing God's work (I Corinthians 7:29–30 TLB).

'But you don't understand,' you say, 'I'm old and tired! I have arthritis, high blood pressure and a worn out heart! I need to rest and just take it easy.'

God says:

> Even to your old age and gray hairs I am He, I am He who will sustain you (Isaiah 46:4).

Think of the long distance runner. At some point he will feel exhausted, but he knows that if he holds on he will reach a plateau where he receives a 'second wind.' Then he is off and running with new energy and enthusiasm.

Isaiah reminds us of what the Lord will do for those who are committed to pressing on to serve God as long as they live:

> He gives strength to the weary and increases the power of the weak. Even youths grow tired and weary, and young men stumble and fall; but those who hope in the Lord will renew their strength. They will soar on wings like eagles; they will run and not grow weary, they will walk and not be faint (Isaiah 40:29–31).

You remember my experience. I was worn out in body and spirit, but then the Lord called me to get back into the race. When I responded with repentance and diligent seeking after Him, He gave me incredible new vitality, strength and joy. Isaiah's prophecy came true within me:

> Arise, shine . . . The Lord has risen upon you . . . Then you shall see and be radiant, your heart shall thrill and rejoice (Isaiah 60:1, 5 RSV).

God offers rewards, not retirement. He promises us joy that no one can take from us, strength for the task, peace in the midst of the storm, a life that is abundant and full, and the sweet Spirit of His abiding presence. He also offers us the reward of eternal life with Him, and a mansion that He is building right now. But there is no retirement on this earth—or even in heaven for that matter:

> Here is a trustworthy saying:
> If we died with him,
> we will also live with him;
> if we endure
> we will also reign with him (II Timothy 2:11–12).

If we are faithful on this earth, we will reign with Christ someday. What an exciting prospect! But if our last years on this earth—our preparation school for eternity—are spent in ease and self centeredness, will we be ready (or even qualified) to reign with Christ? He never stopped doing the will of the Father, never stopped seeking to save and help the lost and hurting, never stopped giving His life away in sacrificial love. We need to follow in the footsteps of our Lord and Master if we want to reign with Him.

Revelations 20:6 gives us a picture of what we are being prepared to do:

> Blessed and holy are those who have part in the first resurrection. The second death has no power over them, but

they will be priests of God and of Christ and will reign with him for a thousand years.

Don't think about, plan on or prepare for spiritual retirement!

Come out of retirement those of you who have already retired. Grow strong in the Lord so that you can continue to do the work of Him who called you out of darkness into His wonderful light. Let's get ready to reign!

God encourages us with His own Words:

> To Him who overcomes and does my will to the end, I will give authority over the nations (Revelation 2:26).

> Let us not be weary in well doing: for in due season we shall reap, if we faint not (Galatians 6:9 KJV).

> Therefore let us not sleep, as do others; but let us watch and be sober. Pray without ceasing (I Thessalonians 5:6, 17 KJV).

> Watch out that you do not lose what you have worked for, but that you may be rewarded fully (II John 1:8).

> The Lord will guide you always: he will satisfy your needs . . . and will strengthen your frame. You will be like a well-watered garden, like a spring whose waters never fail (Isaiah 58:11).

20

A Challenge To Fight The Good Fight

Finally, be strong in the Lord, and in His mighty power. Put on the full armor of God so that you can take your stand against the devil's schemes (Ephesians 6:10–11).

You and I are important to God! His eternal plan awaits the completing of our mission. At times we may not feel important, and we may not even know what it is that we are supposed to be doing. But this is when we need to be the most diligent. We need to find out what it is that we should be doing!

What have our calendars told us about our priorities? They can be most revealing! Has some pursuit, perhaps one of those mentioned in the last few chapters, been more important than serving God and His people? Perhaps some entertaining thing has been robbing hours that might have been spent growing strong in the Lord.

By what criteria do we judge whether a particular pleasure is truly 'for God's glory?' Three hundred years ago, a young man named John Wesley asked his mother that same question. She wrote back to him suggesting these rules for judging whether a particular thing is God's will for us:

'Whatever weakens your reason.

Whatever impairs the tenderness of your conscience.

Whatever increases the authority of the body over the mind.

Whatever takes away your relish for things spiritual.

Whatever obscures your sense of God.

That is sin to you no matter how innocent it may seem in itself.'

When we turn away from those things that are 'sin to us, no matter how innocent they may seem,' we have a chance to grow strong. We know by now, that each decision we make about how much time we spend toward disciplined growth is important. We become strong in the Lord as we meditate on His truths, test His promises, hide His Word in our hearts, and obey His commands with our moment to moment choices. And our spiritual health is vitally important, for we are being called to battle.

Hear the cry of Joel:

> Proclaim this among the nations: Prepare for war! Rouse the warriors! Let all the fighting men draw near and attack. Beat your plowshares into swords and your pruning hooks into spears. Let the weakling say, I am strong! (Joel 3:9–10).

This is a time of spiritual warfare and God wants warriors who will choose to:

> Be strong in the Lord and in His mighty power (Ephesians 6:10).

Soldiers are called to obey their commander. They have no other business. Every minute of every day belongs to their commanding officer.

We are fighting against forces that we can't see, and that makes them dangerous:

> For our struggle is not against flesh and blood, but against the rulers, against the authorities, against the powers of this dark world and against the spiritual forces of evil in the heavenly realms (Ephesians 6:12).

God calls those of us who are soldiers in His army to be united in a common goal—to defeat the enemy.

During WWII our military forces were directed to defeat the enemy by every possible means. But in the

Vietnam war, our generals were told, 'Fight, but don't do what you need to do in order to win!' That sounds crazy, I know, but I was there and I heard many of the unbelievable orders that came out of Washington. Soldiers were not led by their generals, but by political forces. (Who were often led by the media!)

Many of us in God's army may look like we're fighting to win. But we are really being run by the 'political forces' of this world when we indulge ourselves in this world's entertainments. When we refuse to be disciplined soldiers who take orders from Almighty God in regard to sin in our lives, then we are not doing what we need to do in order to win. We are staging a spiritual Vietnam.

When I was a private in WWII, we were taught to recognize the enemy. He wore a helmet that was easily recognizable. When we saw that helmet we fired. When we saw his uniform, tank or airplane, we fired.

God has described our spiritual enemy. It is anything and everything that is against His will. When we see that enemy we are supposed to 'fire'. We are to attack, defeat and destroy God's enemy by using all the spiritual weapons that He has given us. And He has supplied us richly:

> Therefore, put on the full armor of God, so that when the day of evil comes, you may be able to stand your ground, and after you have done everything, to stand. Stand firm then, with the belt of truth buckled around your waist, with the breastplate of righteousness in place, and with your feet fitted with the readiness that comes from the gospel of peace. In addition to all this, take up the shield of faith, with which you can extinguish all the flaming arrows of the evil one. Take the helmet of salvation and the sword of the Spirit, which is the Word of God. And pray in the Spirit on all occasions with all kinds of prayers and requests. With this in mind, be alert and always keep on praying for all the saints (Ephesians 6:13–18).

Once we get into this kind of spiritual warfare we develop a bond with our fellow soldiers and it's easy to pray for them. War unites in a comradeship that is difficult to explain. We will protect, and even lay down our lives for one another. Our warfare is dangerous, and we may be severely wounded, but members of God's army do not seek to hide in a spiritual hospital. We stay only long enough to heal and get back to the front line.

Another thing I observed during WWII was that most rear echelon soldiers had their own code. It was, 'We will support you front line heroes, but we have better sense than you do. You may get the glory, but we will save our lives.'

Many Christians are rear echelon, support soldiers. They want to be on God's side, but to serve Him as far to the rear as possible. They will support the church and do odds and ends of work, but they prefer the more comfortable life behind the battle zone. They obviously do not understand or believe Jesus' unusual law of self preservation:

> Whoever wants to save his life will lose it, but whoever loses his life for me will find it (Matthew 16:25).

Jesus was out in front in every spiritual battle of His day. He told the disciples to follow Him. They did so, but when the battle became too severe they fell back to safer territory. But after Pentecost they moved from the rear up to the front! They were ready to die if need be for the sake of the Gospel.

God needs more front line warriors today as the spiritual war is becoming increasingly dangerous. He needs soldiers whose minds are not detracted by this world's entertainment—soldiers who are filled with the Spirit.

In times of war the rear echelon troops may be able to build fires, sleep in comfortable beds, and eat hot meals; but the man in the trenches has none of these luxuries. He watches for the enemy. He listens for his orders. He knows that if he fails in his job someone may die.

Have you entered into spiritual bonding with God's front line troops? If so, you want to stay with them. You know that God's people need you, and that you need them. You call out to others saying:

> Endure hardship with us like a good soldier of Christ Jesus (II Timothy 2:3).

If you are still a rear echelon troop, you may not have the zeal to get into the thick of the battle where God's troops are fighting His enemy. You haven't experienced the fierce blast of Satan's wrath. In fact, you may not even know that the war is on. We are at war!

Rear echelon Christians have much time to rest, relax and pass the time. They aren't in a hurry to defeat Satan. But God's warriors hear the bugle sound: 'Charge! Defeat God's enemy. Snatch family and friends out of Satan's grasp.'

True, the battle is costly, and it's often hard to stay the course when everyone you know seems to be in the 'rear echelon.' Jesus went into battle alone. He was so determined to give His life that He let nothing hold Him back.

The natural tendency to preserve our own interests tells us to live in ways that are most pleasing to us. That way of living permits us to relax while others are out fighting the good fight. When we are comfortable in home and entertainment, it is easy to shut out the sounds of the battle, but the battle is raging. Satan has stolen control over many parts of our nation that were once strongholds for God's kingdom.

God invites us to be in His service. But He doesn't want people in the front line who are 'lukewarm.' We would be in the way. We would destroy the spirit of 'family' that unites men and women who feel the shaking of the earth as the spiritual battle rages.

Front line, spiritually hot soldiers have a fire in their hearts that urge them forward. They may be tempted to seek the comforts of the easy life, but they are holding on with a tenacity that delights their Commander! He is storing up for them a crown of glory that will never fade away. He is preparing for them a place that is marked, 'Front Line Troops Only.' The Bible calls them 'Overcomers.' And oh, the wondrous rewards He has reserved for those who overcome!

Hear the promises of the Lord:

> To him who overcomes, I will give the right to eat from the tree of life which is in the paradise of God (Revelation 2:7).

> To him who overcomes, I will give some of the hidden manna. I will also give him a white stone with a new name written on it, known only to him who receives it. I will also give him the morning star (Revelation 2:17, 28).

> He who overcomes will . . . be dressed in white. I will never blot out his name from the book of life, but will acknowledge his name before my Father and His angels (Revelation 3:5).

> I am coming soon. Hold on to what you have, so that no one will take your crown. Him who overcomes I will make a pillar in the temple of my God. Never again will he leave it. I will write on him the name of my God and the name of the city of my God, the new Jerusalem, which is coming down out of heaven from my God; and I will also write on him my new name (Revelation 3:11–12).

> To him who overcomes, I will give the right to sit with me on my throne, just as I overcame and sat down with my Father on his throne (Revelation 3:21).

> Now the dwelling of God is with men, and He will live with them. They will be His people, and God Himself will be with them and be their God. He will wipe every tear from their eyes. There will be no more death or mourning or crying

or pain, for the old order of things has passed away. To him who is thirsty I will give to drink without cost from the spring of the water of life. He who overcomes will inherit all this, and I will be His God and he will be my son (Revelation 21:3–4, 6–7).

Ever since we first heard about you we have kept on praying and asking God to help you understand what He wants you to do, and to make you wise about spiritual things. That the way you live will always please the Lord and honor Him, that you will always be doing good, kind things for others, all the time learning to know God better and better. We are praying, too, that you will be filled with His mighty, glorious strength so that you can keep going no matter what happens—always full of the joy of the Lord (Colossians 1:9–11 TLB).

Epilogue

I have read every page of this book dozens of times. Each time I read it, my own resolve is strengthened.

The Scripture verses continue to breathe new life into my spirit.

Your understanding of this message and resolve to serve the Lord will also grow, if you read these pages many times.

The message in this book has the potential to change the course of history as the Holy Spirit awakens us.

Ask the Lord how many Christians should read *Are You Sitting Comfortably?* Then do whatever you can to place a copy in their hands!